"Charlie's financial advice, comedic timing, and stage presence are all brilliant. He went all out in making this a masterclass on how to achieve any dream you have. I was truly inspired by the show and learned a ton. I can't wait for everyone I know to see this show because it will help you think so differently about what making money is all about."

—Nick Nanton
Emmy Award–Winning Documentary Director

"You're going to laugh your head off and have a damn good time. People you show it to will think a lot better of you after the show. You'll see humor in a negative situation!"

—Dan Sullivan
Founder and President of The Strategic Coach Inc.
A visionary, an innovator, and a gifted conceptual thinker

"This will change your life! I was blown away not just from Charlie's performance... this is funny, entertaining, and educational."

—Ron Bradley
Founder and CEO of Auxani Advisors

"Who would have thought that a person could make investing, money management, and retirement not only entertaining but funny? And I do know funny because I actually won an Olivier for best new comedy a few years ago."

—Alan Shorr
Tony Award–Winning Broadway Producer

"Charlie helps you think about the mindsets and what you truly want so that you live the life you've always dreamed about and deserve. I got a *ton* of practical value, and you will too."

—Howard Getson
CEO of Capitalogix

"This isn't like any other self-development program. Charlie shows you how to empower yourself to get what you want right now. It could be lifechanging for you. I know it is for me!"

—Dr. Mark Young
Host of Blunt Force Truth *Podcast,*
Founder of Jekyll+Hyde Labs

"Managing your money to meet financial needs today and far into the future is complex. It can also be incredibly boring! Cue Charlie Epstein. A former comedian, tenured financial advisor, and self-made multi-millionaire, Charlie Epstein's *Yield of Dreams* is the most practical and entertaining financial book I've ever read."

— Adam Witty
Founder & CEO, Forbes Books

YIELD OF

DREAMS

THE KEYS TO LIVING PASSIONATELY

YIELD OF
DREAMS

THE KEYS TO LIVING PASSIONATELY

BASED ON THE ONE-MAN SHOW
WRITTEN AND PERFORMED BY

CHARLIE EPSTEIN

Advantage | Books

Published by Advantage Books, Charleston, South Carolina.
An imprint of Advantage Media.

ADVANTAGE is a registered trademark, and the Advantage colophon is a trademark of Advantage Media Group, Inc.

Printed in the United States of America.

10 9 8 7 6 5 4 3 2 1

ISBN: 978-1-64225-770-0 (Hardcover)
ISBN: 978-1-64225-769-4 (eBook)

Library of Congress Control Number: 2023922535

Cover design by Holly Reed.
Layout design by Matthew Morse.

This publication is designed to provide accurate and authoritative information in regard to the subject matter covered. It is sold with the understanding that the publisher is not engaged in rendering legal, accounting, or other professional services. If legal advice or other expert assistance is required, the services of a competent professional person should be sought.

Advantage Books is an imprint of Advantage Media Group. Advantage Media helps busy entrepreneurs, CEOs, and leaders write and publish a book to grow their business and become the authority in their field. Advantage authors comprise an exclusive community of industry professionals, idea-makers, and thought leaders. For more information go to **advantagemedia.com**.

This book is dedicated to the lasting memory of The Founders:
My father Bob "The Entrepreneur" Epstein and my mother
Peg "The Entertainer" Burtaine.

My father never drank. My mother was all the drink he ever needed.

CONTENTS

FOREWORD

I'm Mike Koenigs. I'm here to introduce you to a brilliant and unique ride into the world of finance and dreams: *Yield of Dreams*. The magician behind this captivating journey is my good friend, Charlie Epstein.

I met Charlie at a Peter Diamandis event and got to experience firsthand his magnetic personality. The man is a confluence of comedian, actor, performer, and most surprisingly, a financial guru. It's a mix of pure magic.

Let's backtrack a bit. When Charlie first introduced himself as a financial advisor, I felt the urge to bolt. I mean, in my experience, most financial advisors rank somewhere between "watching paint dry" and "counting grains of sand on a beach" on the excitement scale. You know, kind of like watching two pieces of chalk make sweet love on a picnic table or the thrilling saga of two slices of moldy white bread.

But then, Charlie happened. He was funny in a way that made you hold your sides, honest to a fault, and steeped in the real-life experience that only added to his wisdom. He's a dynamo of talent and charisma rolled into a bolt of energy that lights up a room. Most importantly, he is one of the most abundance-minded people I've ever met. He always operates from the point of view that there is more for everyone. He's a 10- and 100-times multiplier who lives to serve (and entertain).

After I got to know Charlie and saw the potential of combining comedy, education, and money, I gave him an offer he couldn't refuse: an opportunity to create his own TV show or a one-man comedy play to teach everything he knows about money, rolled up with all of his unique superpowers. Charlie had a dream, a vision to blend finance and comedy.

At first, I had to put together an all-star team that could make that happen.

Fortunately, I had a secret weapon, a young videographer turned comedian who used to work with me. This guy had honed his comedy skills at the Comedy Store in La Jolla and eventually left my team to make it big in comedy. He had connections, knew the right people: the A-listers, successful writers, and standup comedians who had written for TV. They were the team we needed to breathe life into Charlie's dream, turning it into a real play, then a TV show, and eventually, a full-blown movie and documentary.

Soon, I had "the Team." Charlie, my incredibly intelligent integrator, Marissa, me, and three comedians. And we were all in my sunny condo in La Jolla, California, sitting across the street from the Pacific Ocean, about to turn that vision into reality. The mission was ambitious—forty-eight hours to spin Charlie's ideas into a masterpiece. Or at least a first draft that didn't suck.

We worked like mad to pack in as much of Charlie's life into this creation. There were stories of everyday folks who, under Charlie's guidance, had transformed their hard-earned money into well-protected, meaningful investments that give them financial freedom and peace of mind. And then there were the touching stories of his family, his rock-solid foundation. Especially his mom, who had always stood by him, encouraging him every step of the way on his crazy, audacious dream chase. Often with a tall martini (or three) in her hand.

But let's get one thing clear, Charlie's world isn't some fantastical land filled with unreachable fantasies. It's a world where dreams take shape and fly. It's a world where you find a friend who's there to guide you, step by step, through the labyrinth of finance, helping you to make your dreams come true. And a world of financial freedom and peace of mind.

If life gives you a chance to work with Charlie, grab it, seize it, and clutch onto it with both hands. Like now. *Now* now.

So, strap in and get ready for a journey unlike any other. It's going to be wild, hilarious, touching, and real. It will be a ride through the brilliant mind of Charlie Epstein and his dream world that will change not only your world, but your relationship with your significant other, your kids, and the people who matter most. Welcome to *Yield of Dreams*.

STAIRWAY TO "HEAVEN"

Every life has turning points. Those defining moments that divide your life into a "before" and an "after." Those personal 9/11s.

Mine came in the form of a phone call.

"Charlie, it's Marie." Marie Case is one of my oldest continuous, trusted friends. She and I have "traveled many miles together" over the years, let's just say.

"You *need* to come to my house," Marie said.

"Okay. When?"

"Like, now. ASAP!"

Marie lived in Austin, Texas. I lived in Somers, Connecticut. This wasn't a matter of hopping in my car and dropping by her house for tea. Still, Marie was like those old E. F. Hutton commercials to me: when she talked, I listened.

"Why do I need to come to Texas?"

"Because Swami is coming."

"Tell me you didn't just use the word 'swami' in a sentence with a straight face."

"I did."

"And who is this Swami I should drop everything to come see?"

"Swami Kaleshwar. He's one of the greatest gurus in India." Cue sitar music.

"And … ?" I said.

"And … he can ease your pain."

Oh … That.

I immediately booked a flight on the Friday red-eye to Austin. Given the pain I was in, I would have *walked* there if I needed to—that's how desperate I was.

You're probably thinking what I was thinking. Why would someone in his right mind jump on a plane at a moment's notice and fly two thousand miles to meet some Indian guru who allows himself to be referred to as Swami?

Well—assuming I *was* in my right mind—there are two things you need to understand. First, Marie is one of those friends where if she calls and says, "You need to be here," you don't say, "Sorry, this isn't a good time for me." You jump on that plane! I've known Marie for forty-one years at this writing. She is the kind of friend who knows you better than you do. Who calls you "a brother on life's transformational road." Whom you can count on to always have your back and whose integrity and intentions are beyond questioning.

And who counts on you to be the same for her.

So yeah, I wasn't about to tell her I needed to stay home and catch the latest episode of *That '70s Show*.

The second thing you need to understand is the pain I was in. Oh God, the pain. I was at the lowest point of my life—deep in fear, deep in scarcity mentality, out of control, and smack dab in the middle of the most acrimonious divorce I've ever borne witness to. I'd been grilled on the witness stand for six hours by my soon-to-be-ex's thousand-dollar-an-hour shark lawyer who was gunning to take *everything* from me, everything I had worked so hard to create up to that point in my life. I was depressed, dejected, and feeling like I'd lost control of my life. My legal bills were rising in real time, and every time I turned around, I was looking at another notice demanding more financial information, more depositions, more court time. I was burning through my savings and investments; trying to navigate a foreign land of courts, judges, lawyers, and GALs; and feeling like I was Kevin Costner trapped in that movie *No Way Out*.

On a daily basis, my wife would call me and scream on the phone for literally hours. I'd put the phone down, walk away, cook an omelet, feed my two young children, do their laundry, vacuum, read my mail, exercise, and when I came back to the phone, she would still be screaming! I know—crazy, right? Did I say *crazy*?

Most days it was all I could do to get out of bed and go to work. I had a job that required a lot of focus and energy. I was a financial advisor to a very active clientele and was also leading financial workshops around the country as "The 401(k) Coach," making over a million bucks a year doing it (most of which my wife's lawyers were trying to get their mitts on). But it felt like I was living in a fugue state. I would get up in the morning in some strange hotel in some strange city, do my daily yoga and meditation, and then break out sobbing for thirty minutes. Then I'd drag myself into the shower, put on my suit of armor, and march into a hotel conference room filled with a hundred advisors waiting to learn *my* "secret-sauce shortcuts" for success. Ha. My assistant, Marie Forest, would look at me with a knowing smile, hand me my Starbucks grande "bone-dry" coconut cappuccino, and say, "You ready to go?"

And I would smile, grab the microphone, and say, "Show time!" And off I'd go.

Those coaching workshops were my solace, the place I could recover myself.

For the rest of the time, it was as if I were on an amusement park ride that was spinning out of control, and every day I was waiting for the whole thing to rip apart and send me flying into orbit, far out into the universe where no one could find me … and depose me!

That was the state of my life as I arrived at Marie's place on Lake Travis in Austin, Texas—a three-story house that looked like a castle tower—at 1:30 a.m. on a Saturday morning. I crawled into the bed in the guest room of her boathouse on the lake and let the sound of the waves lull me to sleep.

A few hours later, I stumbled my way to the main house, passing a line of people waiting to get into Marie's castle. Curious, I thought. The line stretched down her driveway and all the way down her street. Huh?

Entering the kitchen around eight o'clock, still groggy from my flight, I said to Marie, "What the hell's going on here? Who are all these people in line?"

"It's been going on like this for two days," she said.

"*What's* been going on for two days?"

"They've all come to see Swami."

"Why?"

"To ease their pain."

Marie then informed me that "Swami" would see me at eleven o'clock and handed me a pad of paper and a pen. "Go write down what you want to ask him for. Go, go, go."

I left the castle, silently returned to the boathouse, and sat at the edge of the lake, my bare feet dangling in the water. For two hours I struggled to write down what I wanted. Now, you need to understand that over the previous fifteen years I had become a master at writing down my dreams, goals, and aspirations—and proceeding to achieve them. I'd taught this skill to hundreds of financial clients and to the thousands of financial advisors I was coaching. I was a Master of Goals, a Master of Visualization, a Master of Focused Intention.

But at this pivotal moment in my life—with my heart and guts being ripped out of me in new ways on a daily basis—I was now a "Master of Messes," and every desire I once thought important rang hollow.

Each time I would write down a new goal on the pad, I'd look at it blankly, ball up the paper, and toss it bobbing into the lake. (Environmentalists' time to cringe.)

More success—nah, didn't need that.

A bigger house—had that. Not for me.

A fancier car—not even close.

Travel the world—done that.

Get even with my ex—tempting, but no, not even that.

More money, more time, more freedom, more power—no, no, no, no.

None of that "earthly" stuff mattered to me anymore. I was broken, shattered, exhausted, beaten. I was Ali on the ropes, Foreman pounding away at my soft underbelly ... "rope a dope," and yes, dear reader, I was "the dope"!!!

After two hours of torn pages, coming up empty, my hand seemed to move on its own. It wrote one short, single-syllable word on the notepad. I looked at that word for a long time, letting it sink in, then folded up the paper, stuck it in my pocket, and walked back to "the castle."

By the time I arrived back at the main house, the line of seekers had grown even longer; there must have been two hundred people waiting to see Swami. I stepped into the kitchen, and Marie instantly spotted me and said, "You're next."

Next for what? No time to answer that. Suddenly, I was being whisked past all the patient line-waiters—it wasn't till months later that the significance of this "Disney-speed-pass, preferential treatment" would sink in—and shown to the stairs. "Go up to the third floor," Marie told me, "through my office to the den."

I pressed my hand against the folded paper in my pocket and started up the stairs. Part of me felt like I was walking "the green mile" to the chair on death row. Another part of me felt like I was stepping onto an alien craft that would ferry me away to another universe, never to return.

Both premonitions would turn out to be accurate, in a way. Something *did* die in me that day, something that needed to die, and a whole new dimension of life kicked into gear. A deep change occurred in me that day, a change that would forever alter the texture of my life, lead me to new discoveries and new adventures, spiritual serenity, and the writing of this book.

But I knew none of this as I robotically lifted one foot after the other on those fateful steps. All I knew was that I was in pain, that I was climbing the longest staircase of my life, and that I was about to have some kind of encounter with a weird little Indian guy I'd never heard of. I didn't know why I was there. I didn't know what to expect or how to act.

And I *certainly* didn't think "Swami" could help me with the seemingly impossible goal I'd written down on that folded-up paper in my shirt pocket.

But up the castle steps I ascended, like a knight of old, wondering if the person I would meet at the top of the stairs would be a wizard, a sorcerer, or a court jester.

Step.

Step.

Step …

INTRODUCTION

Hi. My name is Charlie Epstein, which, if you're very clever, you've deduced from the book cover. This is the part of the book where the author—if their name isn't Trump or Streep or LeBron—tries to convince readers they aren't about to waste four hours of their valuable time by reading the pages to come. We like our authors to have book-worthy credentials, right? And short of being a household name, there are only a few acceptable credentials that qualify a person to author a book in the brave new publishing world of the twenty-first century: either you've murdered someone, you've got a PhD in something impressive sounding, you've scored three million likes on your Instagram page, or you've made a gajillion bucks in business.

I haven't killed anyone … that I know of. Yet. I don't have an advanced degree or an advanced Instagram following. But I *have* enjoyed success as an entrepreneur, financial advisor, entertainer, and author. So perhaps that gives me the "right" to ask for your time and cash.

As a financial advisor for over forty-two years, I have built my own successful registered investment advisory firm, Epstein Financial Services, which oversees a half billion assets in 401(k) plans and personal wealth management. I recently sold my practice to HUB International for eight figures and continue to run the company. I have built and sold a successful benefit company. I've been involved in starting a community bank, Nova Bank, in 2008, which we successfully sold, *twice*, to the delight of our shareholders. I'm known nationally as the 401(k) Coach, having coached and trained over ten thousand financial advisors. One of my dear friends, John Scott, a hugely successful 401(k) advisor, is fond of saying, "Charlie is the only person I know who can monetize air!" Oh, and I've authored three books on financial topics.

At my core I have embraced the French economist Jean-Baptiste Say's definition of an entrepreneur, which is "one who shifts economic resources from a lower level of productivity to a higher level of productivity and yield."[1] I'm a strong proponent of creating value for my clients and customers. And myself.

BUT THERE'S ANOTHER SIDE OF ME

I'm also a bit of an oddball in the world of business, an alien. I have another whole persona—that of stage performer. I love the performing arts, and I've worked as a musician, a stand-up comic, and an actor. I've appeared in dozens of stage plays and have been in TV commercials and soaps. I was featured in a one-man show in which I played all seven roles. I played Pop in the *Popular Mechanics* video series. I have my Actors' Equity union card. I've been trained in Shakespearean performance and the Meisner method of acting by some of the best teachers in the business.

---

1   "Entrepreneurship," The Economist, April 27, 2009, https://www.economist.com/news/2009/04/27/entrepreneurship.

All my life I've had my trains running on both these tracks. On track one I love business and finance. I have a natural talent for entrepreneurship that began with my successful lawn-mowing and comic book–trading businesses when I was a kid. I like making money, and I'm not afraid of it. I understand how money works and how it can be a liberating force in human life when we learn to harness its power. I understand, too, the crippling illusions people harbor about money and how these illusions create immense suffering.

On track two I love to light up a room as an entertainer. To me there is no better feeling of aliveness than to step in front of an audience, open your heart, and tap into the room's energy to create a vibrant performance that awakens the human spirit in real time. Sandy Meisner said, "Acting is living truthfully in imaginary circumstances." Done right, it demands a level of honesty, presence, and self-awareness unmatched by any other endeavor I know. When you're standing alone on a spotlit stage, hundreds of eyes fixed on you, revealing a character's authentic human emotions and struggles, with no place to hide, it is utterly exhilarating. The great Sir Laurence Olivier said it best when he said, "Look at me … Look at me … Look at me!"

As you can imagine, the world of theater and the world of finance do not always come together comfortably for tea and biscuits. For much of my life, I treated them as separate pursuits—like twin braids of a rope, connected in some way but still distinct. I'll tell you some stories of those times, such as the period when I was working six days a week in Monmouth, Maine, as an actor for twenty-five dollars a week, then rushing back to western Massachusetts to put in an eighteen-hour day in my financial advising business so I could pay the bills. Reveling in the insanity of it all. Bending time.

In the back of my mind, I always yearned to find a way to bring my twin passions together in a more organic, holistic way.

PUTTING IT TOGETHER

When I became the 401(k) Coach in 2002 (which I'll also tell you about later), I began to experiment with bringing my two separate worlds together. I would fly around the country, "performing" for rooms full of financial advisors. My presentation included a bit of character acting, a bit of stand-up. It was fun and rewarding. But it was only when I came to truly understand and accept my *ministry* in life—to "ease people's pain and suffering about their relationship to money"—that I was able to develop the exciting project I'm currently working on. It's called *Yield of Dreams*. It's a one-man show that asks the questions, "What did you want to be when you grew up?" and "What happened to that promise you made to yourself as a child?"

Borrowing its theme from the movie *Field of Dreams*, the show creates its own genre, which I call "financial theater." It's an evening of entertainment—part stand-up, part stage play, part multimedia event—that makes people laugh while dispelling financial illusions that keep them locked in unfulfilling lives. I'm having a blast performing and developing it, and the show is pure *me*. I'll tell you more about it as we go.

What I'll tell you right now is this: there's magic in doing what you were *born* to do. The reason I wrote this book is that I want you to taste that magic. I want you to discover your own *Yield of Dreams*. I want you to dare to use *your* greatest talents and passions in ways that only you can do. I want you to live each day with an "infectious, spirit-bound integrity for wonderment, joy, laughter, play, and discovery for discovery's sake." I believe we all have unique gifts—and unique *combinations* of gifts—that can serve the world. And I believe the world is hungry for us to bring these gifts forward. True fulfillment comes only from allowing ourselves to become a fully realized version of who we are. Now, more than ever, the world needs 100 percent of you—your wisdom, your grace, and your passion.

WHY DON'T WE DO THIS NATURALLY?

Why don't more of us do this, then? Why don't more of us actually live our dreams? Because we've been sold a myth. And we've swallowed it, hook, line, and sinker.

The myth I'm talking about is the myth of the dream deferred. It is a myth that financial advisors have been selling for years. People believe that if they diligently earn their paychecks and save their resources, they will one day attain the freedom to Do What They Love. In other words, if they put the money first, the dream will follow. But life rarely works out that way.

PUT THE LOVE FIRST

One thing I *know*—with every ray of consciousness beaming from every cell in my body—is that the opposite is true. You must do what you love *now*. Don't defer your dreams till retirement. Unwrap your gifts today. Do so passionately, do so purposely, and the financial stuff will work itself out (with a bit of intelligent planning). And I'm telling you this as a financial advisor.

Life is a dance, a musical number. Not a colonoscopy. The goal isn't to get to the end; it's to participate in the dance *now*. While you still have all your moves. To play each note to its fullest.

In my consulting work, in my books, and in my stage show, I dispel a lot of myths. But one "myth" I have found to be absolutely true is this: do what you love, and the money will follow.

That's what this book is about. That is my fervent wish for you.

THE SHAPE OF THE BOOK

The way I hope to inspire you to join the dance *now* is by sharing some of my life story with you. Not because I'm deluded enough to believe my life is the stuff of legends (it isn't), but because I have learned one thing in my career as an actor: in specifics lie universals. By sharing the real events and details of my life, I can speak to you more truthfully than if I were simply to preach generalities. It is in that spirit that I invite you into my life. Think of this as the Story of How One Man Came to Do What He Loves in a One-of-a-Kind Way. I present it with humility and a deep sense of gratitude that you would allow me to share it with you. I hope I've earned the right, through my own trials and errors, my own fumblings, bumblings, and costly mistakes, to even ask this of you.

In each chapter I will talk about a different period in my life and how I responded to the opportunities and challenges I was faced with, and then at the end of each chapter I'll reflect on some of the principles and insights I learned. I hope something in my life will strike a chord in yours and begin the process of opening your heart and soul to who you really are.

And I hope someday I will have the privilege of witnessing *your* gifts unleashed on the world.

ONE

CHILDHOOD: A DIVINE DISCONTENT

I was born with a "divine discontent," a restless sense that I was meant for bigger things. Maybe that's because I got my first big laugh the literal second I popped out of my mother's womb and could never settle for anything less.

It's true. When my parents were expecting me, their doctor confidently told them they were having a girl. So, they named me Charlotte before I was even born. They had the pink blanket and Kewpie doll all ready to roll. When the doctor pulled me out and held me up, everyone took one look at my equipment and burst out laughing. (Not exactly the *kind* of laugh a male dreams of, but hey, it was better than nothing.) And so they promptly named me Charles instead of Charlotte. My sister, who's six years older than me, was expecting a kid sister and still hasn't forgiven me to this day!

A FUSION OF TWO WORLDS

If you look at my family background, it almost seems as if the two tracks of my life—entrepreneur versus entertainer—were laid down and pulling me in different directions from day one. My mother's side was all about creativity and the performing arts. My dad's side was pure business. And both sides loved what they lived, every day.

My grandfather on my mother's side was Henry Burtaine, a highly artistic chap. He was concertmaster at Radio City Music Hall in the 1920s and an accomplished painter. He was quite prolific. His artwork hung all around our house growing up. Now it hangs in the houses of his six grandkids all over the country. The walls (and floors) of my homes are also adorned with his craftsmanship.

My mother was a gifted singer with an operatic voice. She was talented enough to get into Juilliard. She was on her way to a successful career at the Met when she stumbled on my dad, loitering on the streets of Hartford, Connecticut, and was instantly smitten. In the grand tradition of women of that era, she shelved her plans and became a housewife.

When I entered the world, though, she was still singing opera, straddling both worlds—singing and home engineering. I vaguely remember being four or five and going to one of her operas. But then the burdens of life derailed her. Her brother died of pneumonia when he was forty, and she was left to take care of her aging parents, while also caring for my sister, my brother, and me. She let go of the dream of becoming a professional opera singer.

But she never let go of music. Music lived and breathed life in my house, morning, noon, and night. Brahms, Beethoven, Chopin streamed daily from my mother's Victrola. Mom taught piano too. In our house. To my classmates in school. Her Steinway grand sat right below my bedroom, so every day after school, I would hear the ticking of her metronome and the sound of her voice screeching, "What? You didn't practice again?"

To which the classmate of the hour would reply tearfully, "I've been sick all week."

My mother would respond by blowing cigarette smoke in their faces—yes, she was an opera singer who smoked like a car on fire—and saying, "*I'm* sick of your not practicing. Do it again!"

Mom was "the voice" in my life. Still is, even though she recently passed away. She sang in the choir at my temple. On Jewish high holidays, her operatic voice would fill Sinai Temple, where I attended Sunday school, rising over the organ playing of Prescott Barrows. (Yes, he was just what you picture when you read that name.) She also led the choir at Trinity Protestant Church in Springfield. Mom was an equal opportunity hymn slinger.

My dad, Robert Joseph Epstein, came from a business background. His father, Max Epstein, built a thriving accounting firm in downtown Hartford, Connecticut—Epstein & Company. The most successful Jewish businesses in the area went to Max for accounting and tax advice—Savett Jewelers, Sweetlife ... Max always had a smile on his face, a cigar in his teeth, a black coffee in his hand, and a twinkle in his eye that said *I know the secret of life.*

And he did. I spent half my youth trying to figure out why that man was so damn happy. I once found one of his old tax returns among my father's papers. He was worth over a million dollars when he died. So maybe that played a part. A million bucks was a lot of folding money in the 1960s. But my grandfather's love for life went way beyond money. He loved what he did, every day. Not many people can say they love their work, their wife, their family, their friends, their clients, their congregation, and their community. But Max could.

You see, Max came to this country when he was twelve years old from Russia, where Jews were persecuted in pogroms. Russia held nothing for him but pain and suffering. America was the land of opportunity, and from the time he landed on these shores, he worked every day to embrace that opportunity. No one gave my grandfather anything. He created it all from scratch with his own blood, sweat, and tears. He was that entrepreneur described by Say, who constantly shifted resources "from a lower level of productivity to a higher level of productivity." And when you create something from nothing, the benefits are exponential. Your courage and commitment command respect, and "the world is your oyster!"

One Saturday in 1973, when Max was eighty-one, he did what he always did. He went into the office at eight in the morning and worked till noon. Then he went to the golf course he had founded, ate lunch with his cronies, smoked his cigar, drank his black coffee, and went out and played eighteen holes. That night he went to a party, as he loved to do, in West Hartford, Connecticut, with people half his age. He realized he'd left his cigars in his car, kissed his second wife, Dora (his first wife, Vera, had died of cancer nine years prior), went outside, started across the street, and *smack*—was slammed by a hit-and-run driver and killed instantly. I like to say if he'd had sex that day, he would've done everything he loved on the last day of his life. No regrets, coyote.

My dad inherited his father's entrepreneurial work ethic, went into business, too, and became a shining example of the American dream. A member of the Greatest Generation, he served in *both* WWII and the Korean War as a lieutenant in the army. When he and his buddies came home, they made the conscious decision to forget about the War. They knew their greatest real estate lay in their future—a future they'd been dreaming and scheming about since their days together in

West Hartford, Connecticut, and at Dartmouth College in Hanover, New Hampshire. They considered themselves the "lucky ones" who'd made it home in one piece and were determined not to waste their good fortune. With that in mind, my dad and his two best friends, Charlie Carples and Stanley Vogel, got jobs at Brown-Thomson and G. Fox in downtown Hartford, where they cut their teeth in the "rag business" (retail clothing). But all the while, they dreamed of starting their own clothing stores—which was exactly what they did.

Charlie and Stanley started Casual Corner, a women's clothing store, in 1950. (Remember Casual Corner? At its peak, there was one in almost every mall.) My dad, along with a partner, started Deb's women's clothes on Bridge Street in Springfield, Massachusetts. I think he called his store Deb's because women didn't want to buy brassieres from a store called Bob's.

Retail is a tough business, with long hours, but back then stores were closed on weekends, so that's when dad would be home. He was a classic 1960s weekend dad, mowing the lawn and painting the house, *Leave It to Beaver* style.

After he'd been running Deb's for ten years, his friends Charlie and Stan came a-calling. "Bob, we're going to open a second Casual Corner store in downtown Springfield and move our operations there. Come join us as general manager, and the sky's the limit."

Bob said yes, and the rest is some pretty nifty history. Dad was with the company for thirty-eight years, rising to senior executive vice president of US specialty retailing stores. (Charlie and Stanley sold out to US Shoe for a tidy sum in 1971, and US Shoe later expanded into a larger holding company, US Specialty Retailing.) My dad built and oversaw the entire distribution center and operations for the company in Enfield, Connecticut.

I remember when he retired at sixty-eight, they had an outdoor ceremony for him that lasted a whole afternoon. Employees stood in line for three hours to shake his hand. They even named the pond behind the main office building Lake Epstein and installed a bench with a plaque honoring him. My dad, in his typical self-deprecating fashion, said, "Yeah, and when I'm gone, the geese will be shitting on my name."

I go there once a year to toast him, and, sure enough, those geese love to shit on his name! I swear they store it up for him.

Mom and Dad were very different types of people, on very different inner tracks. My mom was the most beautiful, vibrant, and creative "people person" you can imagine. Full of laughter and energy. She smoked and drank (and almost to her final day at ninety-four consumed enough vodka annually to float a midsized sailing vessel—I'm not kidding!). My dad was a teetotaler. He was staid and straightforward and observational. We called him Steady Eddie, the lighthouse in the storm. My mother was all the drink he ever needed. They were crazy about each other. And their marriage worked.

My parents loved life and expressed their enthusiasm openly. They reveled in hanging out with friends and family. And the parties, holy crap! Everyone was always dressed to the nines—Charlie Carples in his patent-leather white and brown spats, Stan Vogel with his slicked-back Dick Tracy hair, and the women in their bright designer-inspired dresses, looking like they'd just stepped off the set of *Bewitched* or *I Dream of Jeannie*. Everyone with a cigarette in one hand and a drink in the other. Except my dad—he didn't need them. He had my mother instead.

Together my parents carved out a beautiful life for themselves and for my siblings and me. The home they created was filled with love, a wonderful work ethic, and the freedom to discover what we loved most in life. Looking back, I think it was their marriage that gave me confidence that the entrepreneur and the entertainer in me could someday find a perfect union.

THE ACTING BUG

My love of performing was partly due to genes and partly due to my family's particular constitution. I was the youngest, so in my early life, I served as a source of amusement for my brother and sister. Here was one of their favorite routines: every time Mom would go out into the backyard to feed the birds or hang the laundry, they would tell me she had gone away in the car. I would predictably burst into tears, scream, "Baby go baba car mom," and hurl myself at the door, while my dear brother and sister would predictably burst into gales of laughter. Great stuff, I tell ya.

My sister, Debra, was six years older than me, so we didn't really grow up together. The only thing I remember about her from childhood was the back of her head as she ran screaming into her bedroom, the door slamming behind her. And my brother, Paul, though we did some typical bro things together, was a scholarly type. He and his best friend, Brad Rush, were the number one debating team in the state of Massachusetts all their four years of high school. Paul's bedroom consisted of walls of books. Period. He would lock himself in his room every day and just read. And my father, of course, was only around on weekends.

Which left my mother with a *lot* of time on her hands. And Mom had an active mind. She loved to *engage*. I soon learned that Mom would serve as an enthusiastic audience for whatever brand of idiocy I was in the mood to parade. I would tell her jokes, try out new faces and dance moves on her, and do impersonations of people on TV.

She would laugh uproariously and applaud. I couldn't get enough of that laughter and applause.

I took my talents to the classroom, where I also discovered a ready audience for my comic wares. Every chance I got, I was acting out some dumb skit or impersonating some teacher—in the halls, in the schoolyard, in the back of the class. The first time I performed on an actual stage with a live audience was in sixth grade. It was a talent show, and I walked out in my yellow bellbottoms and afro and did Bill Cosby's Noah routine. *Noah … I want you to build an ark.* "What's an ark?" *Get some wood and build it three hundred cubits by eighty cubits by forty cubits.* "Uh … what's a cubit?"

From the moment that audience gave me its first laugh, I was hooked. I knew entertaining audiences was all I ever wanted to do. Laughter was the drug, and I was addicted.

All the way through school, I was the class clown, the rebel without a clue, the rule tester. It was always *How far can I push this joke? How mad can I make this teacher without getting punished? How far outside the lines can I color?* The problem—for the school—was that I was also an A student. And here's the thing: if you're an F student and you're the class clown, you're an easy problem for them. They just kick your ass out. Done. But when you're a top student and you confront your teachers with "You don't know what you're talking about" and you're *right* … well, let's just say you create a special challenge for school principals.

And you sure don't make your own life any easier either. That was the part I didn't grasp.

I actually got detention in kindergarten. No joke. I was such a problem that for twenty-four consecutive school quarters—from first grade all the way through sixth grade—I got a "U" in conduct. And U did not stand for "U gotta see this kid." It stood for unsatisfactory.

I remember, in sixth grade, when I finally got my first "S" in conduct. My father, who was sober as a Mormon judge, went out and bought a bottle of Dom Pérignon and a carton of cigarettes and drank and smoked them all by himself. I was so concerned for his health that I made sure to get a "U" on my next report card just to get him to quit!

It got so bad I was eventually sent to the school psychiatrist. "You become easily vrustrated," he told me in his broken, high-pitched German accent. "Every time you feel zee vrustration mounting, I want you zhould take zees pencil, focus your vrustration on it, and zen ..." *Snap*. He broke the pencil in half.

I tried his method. It wasn't long before I'd burned through my household's entire pencil inventory and everyone at school had learned, *Don't lend your pencil to Epstein.* They were tired of getting them back in two pieces.

I loved to poke sticks at anyone in a position of authority. At home, as I got older, my oppositional nature became focused on Mom. By the time I was a freshman in high school and my brother and sister had gone off to college, my parents and I would sit down at the dinner table, and my father would sigh and say, "Could we *please* just have a quiet dinner tonight?" And I would say, "Sure—as long as she doesn't say anything stupid."

THE BUSINESS BUG

At the same time, though, I was also a budding businessman. I liked making money. I liked it a lot. And I was good at it. But I liked doing it my way. (I guess that's what differentiates an entrepreneur from a corporate Employee of the Month. They both work hard, but the entrepreneur likes to do it their own way. *And* keep all the profits.)

My first money-making enterprise was mowing lawns in the neighborhood. I learned, early on, the art of negotiating my own value, the art of turning a "no" into a "yes," and the art of using OPE—other people's equipment—to build a business. My dad let me use his sit-down lawn mower, and my neighbor, Mrs. Cohen, let me use her power sweeper—provided I agreed to mow her lawn for free.

I'd drive around the neighborhood, steering the rider mower with my right hand and dragging the power sweeper with my left. Needless to say, my business was an all-cash, off-the-books enterprise. No licenses, no taxes, no insurance, no overhead except for gas (and no need for a CPA—sorry, Max!).

So there was no real competition. The professional landscaping companies couldn't compete with me on price. I charged ten bucks for a lawn. My goal was to have ten weekly customers, which would gross me a hundred dollars a week. And I hit my goal in a month, by knocking on doors and selling myself. (Little did I know that, at my young age, I was honing the art of cold calling, a skill that would come back to serve me well in my early twenties.) This was 1971. I was fourteen, and I was killing it.

My other hustle was selling/trading comic books and Marx Brothers movie memorabilia. Buying and selling comic books is like buying and selling stocks or any other appreciating commodity. You want to buy low and sell high. So you need to develop a network of reliable sellers and hungry buyers. You also need to have an instinct for spotting a sound investment. And you need to talk a good game. This is where I learned the art of negotiation and how to use OPM—other people's money—to make more money.

My greatest thrill was when I found myself haggling for *Fantastic Four* number one, in good condition, using thirty dollars I borrowed from my friend Andy Mackler. The seller was trying to get me to pay more than it was worth at the time—it was only in *good* condition, not *mint* condition. I asked him, "Why are you selling?" and he said he was trying to raise money to buy *Spider-Man* number one, a trending comic. I convinced him that my thirty-dollar offer was the best he would get and that if he didn't take my offer, he might lose the opportunity to buy the "only" copy of *Spider-Man* number one available at this particular convention.

What he didn't know was that I had already found a buyer for *Fantastic Four* number one who was willing to pay me sixty dollars. My buyer took my advice, got his money, and happily bought *Spider-Man* number one. I happily sold that *Fantastic Four* number one for sixty dollars, a 100-percent profit. We both got what we wanted. And that's how I began to learn the art of "win-win," abundance-minded negotiation. I also learned a valuable economic lesson: if the "market" believes something is scarce, it *will* pay a higher price.

FREEDOM AND MODELING, THE MAGIC COMBO

I think the reason I learned valuable lessons for success—instead of lessons like "how to sneak a shiv past the prison guards"—was that my parents were wise enough to use a combination of freedom and modeling. That is, they gave me enough freedom to make my own mistakes and discoveries, and they *modeled* principles of success instead of trying to *teach* them to me. I was so rebellious that if they had tried to box me in with rules, I would have smashed their boxes, and if they had tried to teach me lessons directly, I would have made it my sacred duty to disprove them. So they adopted a quieter, more hands-off approach.

The amount of freedom I had as a child and a teenager is hard to grasp in this era of "helicopter parenting." Today's parents seem driven to structure all their kids' free time and make sure they're safety padded and supervised 24/7/365. When I was a kid, your mom basically kicked you out the door on the first day of summer and said, "See you in the fall." My friends Pete and Doug and I were free to spend our entire days doing ... whatever. We knew it was time to go home for supper when the streetlights came on.

My parents allowed me to go door to door drumming up customers for my lawn care business and to attend comic book conventions on my own. To this day I still can't believe that when I was sixteen they even let me and my buddy Andy Mackler go to Manhattan for four days, unsupervised, with Dick Sykes, "the Rebel Peddler," and his one-eyed, redheaded girlfriend. Yes, they did, no questions asked!

My parents and grandparents didn't *teach* us the value of a good work ethic; they *lived* it. Work was in their blood. Work was a way of life. Work was a badge of honor. The unspoken message was that if you worked hard and put in the time and effort, you would be rewarded. And you should *enjoy* the rewards. My folks weren't afraid to spend money on having fun with their friends and family and doing what they loved. They would take the family to New London Beach and the boardwalk and treat us to ice cream and beach pizza. I hated the water, but I loved the penny arcade. I would play Skee-Ball for hours, winning hundreds of tickets, and then spend even more time at the prize counter, buying junk only a six-year-old could love. I had enough glowing skeletons to populate a zombie apocalypse.

My dad loved golf—from the time he was fourteen till the age of eighty, a year before he died—and he indulged his passion at the local country club. (I hated golf but later regretted not learning to play so I could spend time with him. Maybe that's why I took up the game in my late fifties, joining *three* country clubs to the tune of hundreds of thousands in annual membership fees.) My dad became president of Twin Hills Country Club in Longmeadow, Massachusetts, the town I grew up in. He would play every weekend, and I would hang at the pool, learning how to throw a one-and-a-half somersault off the springboard. We lived "the good life," and we knew it came courtesy of hard work. Today, I'm a proud golf-playing member of Twin Hills.

But the greatest examples of the virtues of success were my grandfather Max Epstein and my grandmother Vira. Almost every other weekend, we would visit them at their country club, Tumblebrook, in Bloomfield, Connecticut. I was only four at the time, but I clearly remember Max and Vira holding court. They were the king and queen of the club. Everyone came to visit their table, and we were proud to sit there with them, along with my cousins and their parents.

I was in awe of my grandfather. And being able to walk up to the bar and order as many Roy Rogers drinks as I could slug down? Not too shabby either. I remember, even at the age of four or five, thinking, "Hmm, a person could get *used* to this."

And then there was the famous "back room," where the men would go to play cards, smoke cigars, and drink black coffee. My grandfather would step out of that room, beaming that famous smile, coffee in one hand, cigar in the other. He was the living embodiment of Do What You Love and the Money Will Follow. His passion for the work he did rippled out to every corner of his life, and my father and mother inherited the same beautiful virtue. There were no handouts in my family. No entitlement mentality. You worked hard, and then you benefited from your efforts. And you gave back to your community too.

Work hard, play hard, and create a life worth living—that was the magic formula they modeled. My folks loved to share their trials, tribulations, and conquests with their fellow entrepreneur friends, who were equally unafraid of risking their sweat equity on their belief in themselves. That was the fire hose of life I drank from. Do what you love and the money will follow. Put in the effort. Bank on yourself. Commitment and courage lead to confidence and capabilities. Success leads to greater success. The future is your only real estate.

Full disclosure: I saw the flip side too. Not to a heartbreaking degree, but it was there. My mother *didn't* follow her dreams. In her nineties she talked about this quite a bit—not having gone for it. I think that's why she was so delighted to see me living *my* dreams, refusing to let my doubts and circumstances stop me. It's not that she was bitter about her life. She wasn't. She believed she had done what needed to be done. But of course, she didn't *need* to get married at twenty, with all the sacrifice that entailed back then. That was a choice.

And it was the kind of choice I see clients making every day in my advising practice: putting their personal passion last. Generation after generation continues to make this choice and to teach their kids to make it. It's supposed to be a formula for success—God knows why. But it fails almost every time.

WHAT I LEARNED ALONG THE WAY

As I look back on my early life, I can identify several key principles I was fortunate enough to learn sooner rather than later.

QUESTION AUTHORITY

Don't buy other people's bulls**t.

I've always had a strong antiauthoritarian streak. And it has done me much more good than harm. Admittedly, it was a toss-up for a while there. After all, there are plenty of "antiauthoritarians" serving chipped beef on toast to other antiauthoritarians in lovely places like Sing Sing. But I was lucky enough to turn my antiauthority stance in a positive direction at a pretty young age—I'll talk about that in the next chapter.

Accepting other people's versions of reality is fool's gold. It's been my experience that whenever someone tells us to accept a belief because "that's the way it is" or, worse, "because I said so," there's usually a major hole in that belief.

You are the greatest authority on your own life, not anyone else. And you should always trust your inner compass over the authoritative pronouncements of others. *That's* the skill we should be teaching our kids—honing and trusting their inner compass. When a child questions why they're being asked to do something, parents and teachers should rejoice. They should view it as an opportunity to *sharpen* the child's inner guidance system rather than stomp it out with a "shut up and do as you're told." But instead we view the child's "willfulness" as a disruption. By our words and actions, we demonstrate that we value obedience more than critical thinking or developing a moral compass. As a result, by the time most of us reach adulthood, our inner guidance system has atrophied like a muscle that's never been used.

The people who change the world are the troublemakers. Be a troublemaker.

WHATEVER GIVES YOU ENERGY IS WHAT YOU SHOULD BE DOING

When I was a kid, two things gave me energy—making money and making people laugh. And today I perform a comedy show about finances. Hmm, could there be a connection? Gosh, I wonder.

It's the things that *give* us energy, not the things that *drain* our energy, that hold the secret to what we're here on this planet to do and to give. Often—though not always—these are the things we're talented at too. But even in the case where the talent isn't there, your passion holds the key. Let's say you love golf, but you'll never be the next Tiger Woods. Maybe that means you could be a golf course designer. Maybe you love great writing, but your similes are as clumsy as an inebriated warthog doing a handstand in a rowboat. Perhaps you were born to be a literary agent or a publisher.

If you have two or three (or more) pursuits that give you energy, be open to the possibility that there may be a way to combine them. Don't force the issue or think too hard about it. Just ask your inner guidance (or God or the universe or the magic eight ball …) if there's some way to bring your passions together to serve the world. Allow the answer to come to you in its own time. It may come in the form of a spontaneous insight or an unexpected opportunity.

MODELING IS EVERYTHING

My parents didn't try to *teach* me the rewards of having a good work ethic; they lived it, and by living it they taught me in the only way a person can ever teach anything. Through modeling. "Do as I say, not as I do" doesn't work—in parenting or any other arena. Kids learn from what their parents *do* and from observing the consequences of those actions.

My parents worked hard and thoroughly enjoyed the fruits of their labors. And so I grew up unconflicted about money. I've talked to many, many people, however, whose parents *tried* to teach them the rewards of a good work ethic, but who modeled something different. And so their kids picked up the contradiction, not the would-be lesson.

The surest way to change the world is to be an embodiment of the values you wish to spread. And to do so with an infectious, spirit-bound integrity for wonderment, joy, laughter, play, and discovery for discovery's sake.

. . .

Now I'd like to tell you about how I first started to figure out how the game of life is played.

TWO

THE TAO OF HIGH SCHOOL: IF YOU CAN'T BEAT 'EM, JOIN 'EM

Remember the *meniscus* from the chem lab in high school? It was that curved bit of surface tension at the top of a test tube full of liquid. You could poke the meniscus and bend it out of shape a bit without rupturing it. But if you poked too hard, of course ... *pop*. A practiced meniscus poker could get pretty good at sensing how far to push the membrane without popping it. But still, if you kept messing around, you knew the pop was coming eventually.

That was me as a kid. Always pushing the meniscus to see how far I could go—with a joke, with a comment, with a rebellious act— before the bubble popped, before I received the punishment, the ass kicking, the detention, the expulsion.

Teachers were my favorite *menisci*. I was a pretty smart kid, as I've told you, and had an active mind. And because of that, I had a particular ... *issue* with teachers who didn't know what they were talking about but pretended they did. I took it personally. I felt like they were trying to put one over on me. So if I knew the answer to a math problem or science question and they didn't, I would confront them, right in front of my classmates: "Hey, that's not what Abraham Lincoln actually said!"

Not a formula for success in this world of ours, I admit.

THE GOOD MR. WHITINGHAM

Mr. Whitingham was my English teacher in eighth grade, and I was of the humble opinion that Mr. Whitingham was an idiot. Now, back when I was in junior high, in 1969–1970, English teachers, for some reason, devoted a huge amount of class time and attention to a highly stimulating activity called diagramming sentences. Remember that? It was basically a process of reverse engineering a sentence by laying it out on branching lines and identifying all its constituent elements—subject, predicate, object, adverbial phrase, dependent clause …

It was as much fun as it sounds. The thing about diagramming sentences was you either *got* it or you didn't. The kids in the former group, the ones who grasped the concept intuitively, didn't *need* to work on it, day after day, for three years straight. The ones who didn't get it continued to not get it, year after year. No matter how much practice you gave them. In essence, diagramming was a grand waste of time for all, both the getters and the nongetters.

Well … I *got* diagramming. Mr. Whitingham did not. This man could not diagram his way out of a bag of *See Spot Jump* books. He would do his shoddy diagramming work on the blackboard, and I would walk up to the board and say, "That's not right." And I would erase his diagram and redo it correctly. He would stand there, his blood starting to boil, and then a light would come on in that dark space inside his skull. And he would say, "Oh, um, that's actually right, Epstein."

This habit of upstaging the teacher, needless to say, did not create an atmosphere of mutual warmth and respect between Mr. Whitingham and me. The result was that I began to ignore him and create my own channel of alternative entertainment in the back of the room. One day, toward the end of eighth grade, I was feeling particularly bored with Whitingham and venting my boredom through a series of particularly inventive impersonations. Robin Williams would have been proud of me.

Mr. Whitingham was not. He said, "Epstein, if you don't stop clowning around, I'm giving you a pink slip." Uh-oh. A pink slip meant suspension. A pink slip at this point in my educational career would have been deadly for me. I'd received two of them already, and my school operated on a "three strikes, you're out" policy. So yeah, expulsion was next.

But on that day, for some reason, I threw self-protection to the wind. I became Patrick Henry, I became Mahatma Gandhi, I became that lone student in Tiananmen Square. Consequences be damned, I stood up and said, "You know what would make my day, Mr. Whitingham? If you would write that pink slip. You know why? 'Cause if I have to spend one more minute in this classroom with you, I'm gonna shoot myself in the &%$# head."

There. I'd done it. I'd sealed my fate. I'd opted to die for the cause.

Whitingham wrote the pink slip, as threatened, and I was sent to the office of the vice principal, Mr. Texeira. I knew my goose was cooked. This was my third offense, and I wasn't going to get any clemency from Mr. Texeira. Why? Because I'd already had the exact same type of run-in with my former math teacher, Ms. Dalton. Twice.

Bottom line: I was going to be expelled from school, one month before eighth grade was over.

No graduation. No diploma. My parents were going to love this.

I entered Texeira's office and sat down on the couch—you know, the low one designed to place your pathetic butt about a foot off the ground—and I looked up at his desk, where he sat perched on high like a great horned owl staring down at a three-legged mouse. And I waited for the verdict to be pronounced.

Mr. Texeira surprised me by looking me in the eyes and saying, in a calm but world-weary voice, "Epstein, would you do me a favor?"

I looked around to see if there were any other Epsteins in the room, then gave him the universal *you talking to me?* gesture.

"Yes, you. Would you do me a favor?" Again the calm, world-weary voice. *Favor? What was Texeira trying to pull here?* "Would you just go back to class and *not* act up? Can you do that, Epstein? There's one month left of school. Can you just ... do that?"

I looked up at him and said, "That's it?"

"That's it," he replied.

"Yes," I said to him, my voice uncharacteristically meek. "Yes, I can do that."

And I walked quietly out of the office. I went back to the classroom, and I zipped my mouth.

I knew I had caught the break of a lifetime. And this was one gift horse whose teeth I was not going to examine with dental tools. The Charles Epstein Traveling Circus and Medicine Show had come to a screeching halt.

I graduated from junior high without further incident. And, interesting thing: the school fired Mr. Whitingham, my English teacher, at the end of the year. Because, yes, he really was that incompetent.

But the real turning point, for me, came when I learned that Vice Principal Texeira had been promoted to vice principal at the high school and Ms. Dalton, my math teacher, had become the head of discipline there. So now *both* my old vice principal and my old math teacher, whom I loved to impersonate and who had suspended me twice from junior high, were going to be the Bonnie and Clyde of discipline at Longmeadow High School!

I did the math, as they say. Saw the light. Being a rebellious clown was not going to get me anywhere going forward. Period. And so I flipped the switch. I made a conscious decision: if I can't beat 'em, guess I'll join 'em. And that's exactly what I did.

A NEW LEAF

I decided to embrace high school, to view it as a world of opportunity rather than a prison camp. I learned there were all these cool activities available—complete with equipment and instruction—and you could try your hand at any and all of them. For free. High school became a place for me to experiment, to try everything. It was Playland to me. I signed up for every extracurricular activity I could get my pubescent palms on.

For some reason it didn't faze me when I had no discernible talent in a given activity. I would sign up for it anyway. I tried my hand at several different sports. I was in the jazz band—as the saxophonist, never having played the sax before—and on the school newspaper. Freshman year I went out for football and got elected to student council. I acted in the student production of *Kiss Me Kate*, which my brother produced and his best friend directed. And then, in senior year, I *cowrote* the class play. I got into high school politics too. In freshman, sophomore, and junior years, I was voted class treasurer.

In the back of my mind, I even began to imagine becoming president by senior year.

I had a blast. I wish my own kids—I wish *everyone*—would allow themselves the kind of freedom I allowed myself in high school. It later became a blueprint for my adult life, this idea that "I'm gonna get involved in everything possible and just see what happens."

In the immortal words of my late mother—taken from my *Yield of Dreams* documentary (learn more online at yieldofdreams. live)—"He was the star of everything. He played saxophone in the band. He couldn't blow; it was horrible. I used to say to him, 'Go outside and play; don't practice.' I hated the sound he was making. He was the editor-in-chief of the newspaper. I don't think he ever *read* a newspaper." Thanks, Mom. But you get the idea. I would just throw myself into the middle of things and figure it out from there.

Because of this, I collected a lot of memorable high school experiences. I probably collected more memories in a given year than most people do in their whole school career. But a few stick out in particular …

LEAD IN *MUSIC MAN*

One particularly crazy thing I did in high school was to audition for the lead role in *The Music Man* in junior year. Why crazy? Well, because *The Music Man* was a musical, and I couldn't sing. But I wasn't about to let a trifling detail like that stand in my way. In case you're not familiar with the '50s Broadway hit, it's about a conman and traveling salesman, "Professor" Harold Hill. His scam is that he sells band instruments and uniforms to small-town communities with the promise that he'll provide them musical training as well, and then he skips town after the merchandise has been purchased. Robert Preston won a Tony for playing Harold Hill in the original Broadway production. I figured I was at least as good as Robert Preston.

I remember auditioning. It was a Friday, and it came down to me and another guy. He could sing but couldn't act; I could act but couldn't sing. Getting the part would be a big deal for me, because I would need to give up playing lacrosse if I got it. And I loved lacrosse. Well, the directors couldn't make a decision, and so the other guy and I had to wait until Monday to find out who got the part. It was one of those agonizingly long weekends where you can't think of anything else, but there's not a thing you can do to help your case. You can't exactly call the music director at home and say, "Would a crisp Ulysses S. Grant help you decide?"

I got the part. And if I do say so myself, they made the right decision. When it comes to live theater, always go with acting talent first. A good actor can carry a show and make you forget the fact that he can't sing or dance. It doesn't work the other way around.

My brother was in the audience one night, and at intermission the guy sitting next to him, a complete stranger, turned to him and said, "Man, can that kid act. Too bad he can't carry a tune in a bait bucket." But you know what? Robert Preston couldn't sing either. It's all about mastering the patter and throwing a little musicality into it—"Well, ya got trouble, my friend, right here. I say trouble right here in River City …"

The show was a hit. And a *workout*. Man. Every performance put me through the wringer. But I'd never felt so alive and engaged. I knew I had found the thing I wanted to do forever.

CLASS PRESIDENT

Running for class president in my senior year is another thing that stands out in my memory. The whole thing was surprising in a couple of different ways. The gal who had been the president the prior two years was running for reelection. And she was a shoo-in. No one wanted to run against her. And so my oppositional nature came to life. I decided to throw my hat into the ring. I figured the odds were stacked against me, but I campaigned anyway. I put up the posters and stood behind the table in the lunch hall, hawking my ideas for political and social reform.

When the vote came in, I whupped the incumbent soundly. She never spoke to me again. I remember my mother saying to me, a week or two after the election, "I heard they elected a new class president at your school. Do you know him?"

"Yes," I said to her, "I know him pretty well, as a matter of fact." I'd never even told her I was running.

Looking back, I think what helped me win was that I was involved with a lot of different groups. There were the jocks, and I was *sort of* one of them, but not really. There were the potheads, and I hung out with them sometimes, even though I never smoked weed at school. I was also in with the geeks, the theater kids, the newspaper kids; I moved in a lot of circles. I never *identified* with any particular group, so in that sense I remained an outsider. But by being involved in so many activities, I had backed my way into the center of everything. The quintessential outsider had somehow become the insider. (Bill Clinton, eat your heart out!)

There was a lesson in there somewhere.

Charlie Epstein, perennial troublemaker and class clown who nearly got expelled from middle school, was now the official leader of his class. And he'd gotten there with no game plan except to follow his passions. I liked that.

HURDLES

The experience that sticks with me the most from high school was taking second place in the state high-hurdles competition. Second place? Who brags in a book about taking second place? I do. Here's why …

Just three weeks before the big event, I wiped out in a track meet and destroyed my knee. I actually wiped out *twice* in the same meet, on both the low and the high hurdles. I was new at the high hurdles, so my failure was nothing to be ashamed of. At least that's what I tried to tell myself. But my parents were at the meet—the only time they'd ever come to see me compete—and I was embarrassed by my performance. I wanted to redeem myself.

The obvious decision at that point would have been to quit. After all there were only two meets left in the year—the valley championship and the state championship. And I had just humiliated myself *and* wrecked my knee. There was no way I would be ready to run in the valley meet, which was only two weeks away. And if I didn't run in the valley—and *place* there—I wouldn't be running in the state. So crawling away in ignominy was my only logical choice. And I had a built-in excuse: my ruined knee.

But I didn't make the obvious choice. I didn't take the excuse. I wanted to go out on a high note. I wanted a win. And it's not an exaggeration to say my decision changed my life.

As I said, it was about two weeks until the valleys, and I was on crutches that whole first week. My knee was blown up like a bowling ball. Every day after class, I would go sit for an hour in this piece of Barney Rubble technology—a big oval canister, made of metal, with a whirly thing on one end that looked like a milkshake blender. They called it whirlpool therapy. I think it was about as effective as leeching. I heated and iced my knee daily, and someone with medical training even went into my knee with a needle once or twice. I went through physical therapy too. That was tons of fun, as I recall. For the entire first week, I didn't even know if I was going to be able to run again—I don't mean in the competition, I mean *ever*.

And then, a week before the valley championships, I tossed the crutches aside. I limped out to the training track, and I set up one hurdle. And I spent all day just running over that one hurdle. I would practice springing out of the blocks and jumping that first hurdle, over and over. Fighting through the pain. The next day I put up *two* hurdles and practiced running out of the blocks and over the first *two* hurdles. Over and over. Third day there were three hurdles. Fourth day four. Fifth day five. And then it was time for the meet. I never got a chance to run all ten hurdles in practice.

Now, it happened we had a guy on our team, Jeff Pezza, who was a junior when I was a senior. He was the state champion high hurdler in Massachusetts his freshman, sophomore, and junior years. He was The Guy. And I wanted to learn from The Guy.

Something else you should know about me is that up until my senior year, I had never run the high hurdles. As a matter of fact, I had never run track before my senior year. And when I did decide to go out for track, Coach Williams, the sprinting coach, had me running the hundred-yard dash. For one reason: I was fast. I finished first place in my first two races! In my third race, I glanced out of the corner of my eye just before crossing the finish line and lost. Coach Williams chewed me out for "looking." Sprinters will tell you that "looking" is the kiss of death.

I told Coach Williams, "I'm bored running in a straight line." He said, "Well, what do you want to do?" I looked across the field at Jeff jumping over the hurdles and said, "That!" So with one-third of the season over, I started chasing the best hurdler in the state. And with every meet, I got closer and closer to beating him. And now, with two weeks off trying to get my knee back in shape, and my confidence up, I was going to have to learn from him in real time—*during* the valley meet. And that's exactly what I did. I glued my eyes to Jeff and did whatever he did. Early in the race, he was about three seconds in front of me, which is an eternity in track. But I just kept watching him and mimicking his techniques. And by the time we crossed the finish line, it was a one-two photo finish. He beat me by something like a tenth of a second.

A week later we went to the state meet, and once again crossed the finish line in a one-two photo finish. Jeff beat me by one one-hundredth of a second. He took gold, and I took silver!

I've never been prouder to be second best. I learned so many enduring lessons from that experience—lessons about getting back on the horse, about sucking up the pain, about digging deep inside yourself, about being persistent, about breaking big problems down into bite-sized pieces, about making your way to the finish line one (literal) hurdle at a time. Later in life I would come to call this "incremental progress." For now it felt like bliss, heaven, and pure joy.

I didn't learn those lessons intellectually; I learned them in my cells and bones. I still remember the pain I was in. I remember the exhaustion I had to push through. I remember that feeling of wanting to give up. I remember looking at that hurdle that first day back on the training track and thinking, "That thing is twelve feet high; there's no way in hell I'm getting over that." But doing it anyway. Over and over.

So that silver medal, yeah. Don't tell me it isn't gold.

COMIC CONVENTION

Not all my memorable teenage adventures took place at school. One experience I'll never forget was attending a four-day comic book convention in New York City at the age of sixteen. I mentioned this earlier. The crazy thing is that I did it wholly unaccompanied by responsible adults. It was me, my buddy Andy Mackler, Dick Sykes, a.k.a. the Rebel Peddler, and his one-eyed, redheaded girlfriend. And my parents allowed it. Yes, they did.

As I mentioned earlier, I dealt in comic books and Marx Brothers memorabilia as a side business, and the event we attended was the Comic Art Convention. It was the precursor to today's mammoth Comic Con, and it was the mecca of the comic book world. I think it cost four bucks to get in, but it was free if you had a room at the hotel, which I think was nineteen bucks a night. At Penn Station. In Manhattan. Yup, that's how old *I* am.

It was a huge event. You could buy and sell comics, obviously, and when you weren't busy ogling first editions of *Superman* and *Batman*, you could ogle *people*: hippies, geeks, midnight cowboys, drag queens—we definitely weren't in Kansas anymore. I remember buying *The Fantastic Four*, volume one, for thirty bucks and thinking I was crazy. But feeling euphoric.

We'd save our appetites for our one meal a day at the famous (infamous) Tad's Broiled Steaks on Forty-Second Street. I think it was $3.29 for a T-bone steak, baked potato, salad, garlic bread, and a Coke. The meat required some heavy sawing and chewing, but it tasted like filet mignon to a sixteen-year-old turned loose in the Big Apple. We were in heaven—trading comic books by day, bopping around Times Square by night. If you were alive in 1973, you may recall what Times Square was like in those days. They called it Slime Square. It wasn't the Disney Store and M&M's World and the Olive Garden, like it is today. It was Sodom and Gomorrah. Massage parlors, X-rated book-stores, strip clubs, liquor stores, theaters offering wholesome family fare like *Nymphos in Bondage*. Sex workers and drug dealers. Pimps and mobsters. Druggies and pickpockets and street hustlers.

It was awesome.

I remember smoking my first joint on that trip and watching *2001: A Space Odyssey* stoned out of my mind, lying on the carpeted aisle floor of a massive theater. I also remember being sweet-talked by an attractive sex worker in a tight red dress at the Dunkin' Donuts bar and feeling my resistance to her weakening by the minute. Until I noticed the stubble on her face.

When I think back on that trip, I'm shocked my parents let me do it. No parent nowadays would let a teenage kid loose for five minutes in an environment like 1973 Times Square. And I was there for *four whole days*. Were my parents neglectful to let me do this? Maybe a little. Am I upset at them in retrospect? Hell no. I'm grateful. I think they knew that some adult freedom would be good for me at that age. I *grew* on that trip, let me tell you.

Today's parents are overprotective of their kids. They don't allow them to go anywhere near the *edge* of life, where they might be able to sharpen their survival skills and learn to take care of themselves. Sometimes young people *need* to go into the danger zone. At least *I* did.

WHAT I LEARNED ALONG THE WAY

For many people, high school is a series of embarrassments and "shoulda-dones" that they spend a lifetime trying to forget. For me it was a launching pad. It taught me ...

RIDE THE RIVER IN THE DIRECTION IT'S GOING

One of the biggest lessons I learned in high school was to stop fighting *against* life and go with its natural flow. What a revelation that was!

Once I gave up the knee-jerk rebelliousness of my tween years, I began to see that life is a river, and it is moving in its own direction with its own momentum. You can row against the current if you want. And this may give you the temporary sense that you are the boss of things. But bucking the current is exhausting, and ultimately you lose.

Conversely, when you lift your oars out of the water and let the *current* do the bulk of the work, life carries you further and faster than you could go on your own. And any energy you expend is magnified and amplified by the current instead of canceled out.

When I decided to ride the river in the direction it was going, I discovered there were endless opportunities just waiting for me to step into and utilize for my own creative purposes. There was a school newspaper with its own printing capabilities, distribution network, faculty advisor, and support team. All I had to do was write. There was a theater program with its own stage, lights, costumes, and budget. All I had to do was *act*. There was a football program with uniforms, coaches, a stadium, and a schedule of games. All I had to do was run faster than the guy next to me. A band with free instruments and instructions. All I had to do was "blow." All this structured energy, already flowing forward. And all I had to do was tap into it and *use* it.

Every day, I meet people who spend their lives locked in resistance to *what is*. They hate their jobs, they hate their economic situations, they hate their marriages or their neighborhoods. And they wake up every morning and renew that resistance. Such resistance is not only exhausting but also self-defeating. Any *jiu jitsu* student will tell you that resistance only creates counterresistance. When you fight life, life fights you back. You make enemies, you create new problems.

When you flow with the Tao of life, however, you accumulate allies, and most of your "problems" dissolve on their own.

ONE HURDLE AT A TIME IS THE KEY

The lessons I learned in the hurdles competition are still fresh and alive in my life. The main one is this: virtually any goal is conquerable if you break it down into small, doable steps.

Whenever we are considering a worthy goal—whether it's to succeed in business, learn to figure skate, write a novel, win an election, or play the violin—it can seem unattainable. We look at where we are now and we look at where we want to be, and the gulf between the two seems overwhelming. "There's no way I can do that" is our natural reaction.

Unfortunately, many people quit at that point. They allow the gap between where they are now and where they dream of being to defeat them before they even start. The amount of energy required to reach the goal seems too much to summon. And it is. After all, you can't run a marathon on day one of training, when you're in poor condition and forty pounds overweight.

But you *can* run a half mile. And then a full mile. And then five miles. You *can* do a little bit more than you're doing right now. And each day, each week, you can do a little more than that.

One reason I became a financial advisor is that I love showing people that big financial dreams *are* achievable—if you break them down into small steps and do those steps with consistency. *Compounding* is the magic key, and it works in all endeavors, not just with money. By that I mean each step forward you take grows your capabilities. You gain more resources, more energy, and more strength than you had yesterday. And from that position of greater strength, you are able to accomplish more than you could before, using the same level of effort.

That's the part we can't see at the beginning. We don't realize that, through compounding, our efforts will begin to build on themselves and multiply exponentially. Momentum will kick in.

When we're at the start space of any endeavor, we don't need the energy to *finish*. We only need the energy to *start*. And from there we only need the energy to take the next step. And then the next. Pretty soon we're not pushing anymore; we're being pulled toward the goal. Momentum is doing most of the work. But we need to start first.

BETTER TO ASK FORGIVENESS
THAN PERMISSION

Probably the greatest lesson I learned in high school is to just dive into things. Don't worry about whether you can *do* the thing or not. Don't worry about what others will think of you, whom you might offend, or how much better other people's skills are than yours. Also, don't worry about *how* you're going to pull it off. You'll figure out "the how" once you dive in.

We humans don't do our best learning in a vacuum. We learn when we *need* to learn. And there's no better way to spur that need to learn than by jumping in. We absorb new learning with much greater efficiency when we're already in the deep end of the pool, trying to swim. And we absorb it in a practical, usable way, not an abstract, intellectual way.

What I've also discovered is that when I jump in and commit to something unfamiliar, it forces me to seek out people who know more than I know and have skills I don't have. This, in turn, forces me to learn how to collaborate, how to delegate, how to build teams, and how to deal with different kinds of personalities.

Caution is overrated. When we give too much forethought to trying something new, our minds build obstacles. We begin to tell ourselves all the logical reasons why we shouldn't be trying such a thing. We start to lower our expectations and prepare for roadblocks. And sure enough, those roadblocks appear, right on schedule. It's often better to jump in before we have time to think of all the reasons we're guaranteed to fail. That's what "beginner's luck" is all about— getting great results because you haven't yet learned all the reasons you're supposed to fail.

I'm not saying that you should try to fly a 737 or perform brain surgery without training. (Fortunately, there are safeguards in place to prevent such things.) But whenever it's a situation where the risks are nonlethal, take the dive. Jump in. Figure things out from the inside, not the outside. If you step on people's toes, apologize later.

But don't ask permission first; you'll only be discouraged from even entering the arena.

FAITH

One last thought: you gotta have "faith," people. When those doubts erupt in your mind. When your whole world comes into question. When that "little voice" in your head screams, "Who the f*ck do you think you are? Don't you know you're not good enough?"

My prescription is to tame that "hairy monkey" screeching in your brain. How? Look in the mirror, smile, and say, "Thank you for sharing." And then blast out of the starting gate into that bigger, brighter future you want, and carry that "bitch" across the finish line with you. That takes faith—and guts and heart … and the Mother Divine, who will shine her grateful light on you for your willingness to risk who you are now … for who you can become.

Faith!

THREE

COLLEGE: FULL SPEED AHEAD ON TWO TRACKS

When I think back on my college career, I realize it was bookended by two questions, both posed by my father. Both questions were deceptively simple and straightforward—my father was, after all, a straightforward guy—but both shaped my life in pretty profound ways. The first of these questions, posed in the middle of my freshman year of college, was this:

"What is your major going to be?"

Pretty simple question, right?

NO READY ANSWER

You might think a guy like me—high school class president, honor roll, Mr. Extracurricular Activity—would have put a lot of thought into that question before being asked by his dad. But nope; it blind-sided me. Almost like someone asking me, out of the blue, what kind of funeral I was planning to have. "Um … gee, guess I hadn't really given it that much thought."

You see, my entire approach to college had been a bit scatter-brained. I just didn't put the appropriate amount of planning and attention into it. I had been so *busy* in high school, I think I was actually a bit exhausted by the time I hit senior year. I hadn't learned to pace myself yet. I'd been burning the candle at both ends for years. And I think part of me was kind of done with it all. I was even thinking about enlisting in the army, just to do something that wasn't school.

I did have goals. Fuzzy ones, admittedly. I knew I wanted to be a performer, and I think I was hoping for a little encouragement from my mother, who'd been my biggest fan and who herself had gone to Juilliard. I was hoping maybe she'd tell me to apply to a college of the performing arts. But she was oddly silent on the issue. (Many years later my mother shared with me that she didn't want to push me in that direction, because her father had done that to her. Had I known that was her reason, I might have handled the college application process differently.)

I ended up choosing my college in a sort of passive way. My sister had gone to BU, and I didn't want to follow in her footsteps. Both my father and brother had gone to Dartmouth, so I didn't want to go there either. Didn't need *those* comparisons. A cousin of mine went to Colgate, and one day my parents said to me, "You should apply to Colgate. Lisa goes there, and she seems to like it."

Fine. I applied to Colgate University, among a few other places. It turned out that of all the schools that accepted me, Colgate was the best. It was a good liberal arts school, geographically far enough away from home to give me some independence, close enough that I could go back to western Massachusetts for weekends whenever I wanted.

And so Colgate emerged as the more-or-less obvious choice. I ended up going there more by default than by passion.

Don't get me wrong—Colgate is a great school. I'm glad I went there. In retrospect, the education I got there was invaluable. But at the time I entered college, I didn't really know what I was doing. My first semester was really about feeling out college life in general and checking out the theater possibilities—and the girls and the beer-and-pizza joints and the parties. When I went home for the holidays after that experimental first semester, that was when Dad sat down with me and popped that rudest of all questions: "What is your major going to be?"

Majoring in theater would seem to be the obvious choice for someone like me, but, alas, I hadn't had the foresight to choose a school that actually *offered* a theater major. And my father probably would have vetoed that choice anyway. At Colgate, however, you could *minor* in theater. But only if you majored in English. So that was what came out of my mouth in answer to my dad's question.

"I'm going to be an English major and minor in theater."

It felt very adult and responsible to make such a definitive choice aloud. I was ready to light a cigar and pour myself a brandy. My father, though, looked at me as if I'd just said I was going to major in clowning with a minor in feminist studies.

"Yeah, that and ten cents will get you a cup of coffee," he said, staring at me in open disbelief.

His words cut to my soul like a chill wind. So much for the cigar and brandy. I *immediately* flip-flopped and heard myself saying, "Okay then, I'll be an economics major."

What? From English and theater to economics in one point nine nanoseconds.

My father approved of my new choice, and that was that. I made a decision at that moment that I would major in economics.

… But I would *live* in the theater.

Little did I know what a life-shaping decision that would turn out to be.

MAJORING IN ECONOMICS, LIVING IN THE THEATER

In my four years at Colgate, I did exactly what I set out to do: I majored in economics, but I spent all my nonclassroom time in the theater. In the beginning I would take any role in any show I could get into, whether it was in the university theater or the student theater. Walk-on butler with one line? I'll take it. Third dead Norwegian soldier? Sign me up.

Before long, though, I was getting all the leads.

I ended up performing regularly with a woman whose name, believe it or not, was also Epstein. We were the Tracy and Hepburn of Hamilton, New York. With the billing of Epstein and Epstein, people would have undoubtedly assumed we were married, but she'd already chosen a stage name for herself: Ivy Austin. Ivy was the real deal. When she arrived at Colgate, she was already a member of Actors' Equity. Her father was the musical coordinator for *Sesame Street*. Her uncle was Billy Crystal's manager. Ivy was what you call a triple threat: she could sing, dance, and act. And she was funny as hell. I was a one-and-a-half threat. I could act, and I was funny. But together Ivy and I got the leads in all the shows. Unlike Ivy, though, I had no one coaching me; I was running on raw instinct. But theater in college was a terrific experience.

There were some memorable high points. I directed and acted in a show called *Line* by Israel Horowitz. It was this avant-garde play about people standing in line, and they go crazy and want to kill each other to get to the front. In my freshman year, I took January off and worked at a dinner theater in Windsor, Connecticut. George Chakiris was there, appearing as Sky Masterson in *Guys and Dolls*. Chakiris was a guy who'd won an Oscar for *West Side Story*, and here he was performing at a local dinner theater in the round. I felt kind of bad for him. But he was a true gentleman, an elegant and gracious man.

I also got to spend three days around the great Imogene Coca when she was doing *Once Upon a Mattress* there. I learned a ton from her in those three days.

I got my first taste of romantic relationships at Colgate, too—though a taste was really all you could call it; I was pretty clueless about women (and remained that way for *much* longer than I care to admit). In my sophomore year, I met a gal who was a year younger than me. We were in *Guys and Dolls* together, and we "went steady" for almost three years. When I graduated she dumped me to go back to her old boyfriend. That old tale. Thank the Lord. For both of us.

On the economics side, I learned a lot too. The truth is, here I am today, forty-three years in the financial business, and a lot of what I teach my clients is what I learned at Colgate. I learned the "value" of money and how capitalism creates an environment where anyone with a good idea can find capital to invest in that idea, build a company, and create success—not only for themselves but for their employees and investors. Just ask Warren Buffett or Elon Musk.

What I really appreciate, though, looking back, is that my Colgate teachers taught me *how to think* and how to develop and defend a point of view. Nowadays, it seems college teaches you how to be offended and how to *avoid* hearing points of view that differ from your own. I learned how to break down and analyze ideas and how to refute falsehoods. I learned how to pull together knowledge from different disciplines—which is what I do now in my *Yield of Dreams* show. I learned intellectual rigor.

I had this great philosophy teacher, for example. She was an ex-nun, and she taught American philosophy. Her assignment was always the same: every week we would read a new American philosopher, and she would give us one question. You had to answer the question as if you were that American philosopher. Your answer had to be 750 words. And if you went over by one word, you got an F. I never worked so hard in my life for an A-minus!

Where I learned the most in college, though, was through the travel opportunities. Nothing educates the mind and soul like experiencing life in a different country.

TRAVELS ABROAD

At Colgate the course schedule was what they called a four-one-four. For fall semester you took four courses, then you took one course in January, and then you took four courses in the spring. But in January they offered this thing called Jan Plan (hey, this *was* the '70s). You could do whatever you wanted in January as long as it was approved by a professor.

My economics advisor, Hugh Pynchon, decided to take thirty of us to Canada for the month. We lived at the Y in Ottawa, and we would ice-skate up and down the canal in the freezing cold. Every day for the course work, Pynchon would introduce us to one of his colleagues. These were all people he had gone to school with. They were all either in parliament or were successful entrepreneurs. And we would sit around and engage with these high-level people for hours. What a huge learning opportunity that was.

The best part of the experience was getting to spend time outside the America-centric point of view. I love America, but if we were to go see a shrink as a nation, we would be diagnosed with narcissistic personality disorder. We tend to think we're the be-all and end-all and that the entire world revolves around us. And so here we were in Canada at a time when that country had a huge collective chip on its shoulder about the US, and boy did we get a different perspective. Turns out, people in other countries have a pretty good quality of life and even have some freedoms and opportunities we don't have in America. Who knew?

My Colgate professors were committed to actual learning, not just forcing us to memorize facts and spit them back. Thank God.

The next year, I had a chance to live in London for a semester and a half and study at the London School of Economics (where Mick Jagger had gone). I had never lived in a major metropolitan city in my life, and that alone was a liberating experience. The classes were good, but the city of London, wow! The double-decker buses, the throngs of people, the arts, the night life … the theatre!

I remember the first time I rode "the tube," I saw these people playing guitar at every subway stop. A light bulb went off in my head, and the first chance I got, I took my guitar into the underground. I didn't know what I was doing; I was just wandering around, and I passed this guy playing guitar. He said, "Hey mate, you looking for a pitch?"

Pitch? I had no idea what a "pitch" was. Turns out it's a place where you set up and play and where people pitch their coins into your hat or your guitar case.

"Eddie'll be back in about an hour," he said, "and I'm gonna go take a leak. Why don't you play here for a bit?"

So I did. I started strumming and singing. Now, I told you that I didn't have a voice for singing on stage. That was true, but I could croak out a Dylan tune pretty well—not an amazingly high bar, I admit (sorry, Bob). Pretty soon the bottom of my guitar case was lined with shillings. Eddie finally showed up and said, "Hey, this is my pitch."

You didn't mess with another guy's pitch, I learned. So I left and found my own pitch and immediately found myself making about ten quid—ten pounds—an hour. In 1977 that was about twenty bucks an hour—at a time when the US minimum wage was less than $2.50.

Do the math. I was making bank. And having a blast doing it.

What a great time that was—living in an apartment in London, taking a couple of classes, busking my lungs out in the subway, and lining my pockets with gold. Almost every night I would go see a show in London's West End, either alone or with friends. How could we afford to do that? Here's how: you'd buy the cheapest seat in the house—one quid, nosebleed seats, third level. And just before the lights came down, you'd scan for empty seats. There were always a few no-shows or unsold seats—in the boxes or in the orchestra—and you'd grab them. I must have seen fifty or sixty shows in London that year. Livin' the dream and feeling invincible.

I had a rom-com moment in London too. One night I was on the subway, on my way home from busking. This really cute gal got on the train, and my heart started "squirming like a toad," to borrow a '70s phrase from Jim Morrison. *Say something to her,* I urged myself over and over again. But of course I didn't. The train stopped, and she got off. I had to get off, too, to make a connection to another train. I found myself walking behind her, and she started to go up a staircase. Finally, I blurted out, "So, where in America are you from?"

She turned and looked at me. "How do you know I'm American?"

"Lucky guess," I said. The truth was, she *screamed* American, but I didn't tell *her* that. Turned out she went to Bates College and knew this guy I went to high school with. We hooked up. Hitchhiked to Stonehenge together, had some fun. Nothing really came of it, but it was one of those crazy, magical things that happen when you're young and free in a big, strange city.

THE ENTREPRENEUR EMERGES

I almost stayed in London and didn't come home. Here's how that almost came about.

My biggest problem as a busker, you see, was that I couldn't remember the words to the songs.

Now, it happened there was this music store around the corner from where I lived, near Madame Tussauds wax museum (Baker Street tube for you Londoners). The first time I went in, I started leafing through the albums and discovered there were no records inside the sleeves. All the vinyl was behind the counter, like game disks in today's video game stores. If you were interested in an album, though, you could go up to the counter and ask to hear a sample. And they'd play it for you.

Eureka—the answer to my problem! I started going in and asking them to play all the songs I needed the lyrics for. And as the song played, I'd write down the words on paper bags. Some of the artists, like James Taylor, made my life easier—they would publish the lyrics to their songs inside the album jacket.

One day I was standing at the counter, and I had about five albums pulled out—Crosby, Stills, and Nash; Cat Stevens; Carole King—and I was writing down all the words. This Scottish guy behind the counter kept staring at me and getting progressively more irritated. He finally walked up to me and was about to say something, but I headed him off at the pass. "Hey, you need any help at this store?"

"What?" he replied.

"I'll work here for free."

Here was my thinking. We had no record player in our apartment. If I could work at the store just one afternoon a week, I could listen to all the new music I wanted, plus grab some lyrics. Also, they had a health food store upstairs. Maybe my bosses would throw in a free meal too.

Scottish guy looked at me for about five seconds, then said, "Nobody works here for free, mate. We'll work something out."

And just like that, he took me on. I convinced him to pay me in albums, not cash, and ship them back to the US. I think I got about seventy albums out of the deal, along with all the lyrics I needed for my thriving busking business and free food from the store upstairs.

Gotta love the barter system.

About a month into my "employment," the owner of the store showed up when I was working my shift. He was from Germany, and, as it happened, I'd taken six years of German in high school and college. So I started pattering with him in jive German. He was surprised, and we hit it off right away. I told him about playing in a jazz band in high school, and it turned out he had a secondhand jazz music store up the road on Tottenham Court. Right there on the spot, he offered me the job of managing his other store.

This was my ticket! I could stay in London! Sing in the subway! See shows! Have big city adventures!

Before I knew it, I found myself on the phone with my father. "I don't think I'm coming home, Dad. I don't think I'm going to finish college."

The silence on the line was thundering. "Dad? Hello? Dad?"

Dad proceeded to inform me that I could work in the store until my London courses were over, and then I could bloody well come home and finish my education.

I was an independent adult now, though. I counteroffered with, "Okay, Dad."

LONDON CALLING

I came back to the states. But I wasn't done with London yet. Not in my mind. Once back on US soil, the only thing I could think about was making enough money to go back to London for senior-year Jan Plan. This next trip, I planned to go with a Colgate professor who was a world-renowned Shakespeare scholar. I figured we'd spend a month reading Shakespeare, going to Shakespeare plays, drinking Shakespearean beverages ...

For the time being, though, because of the odd scheduling of my London year, I had half a semester off, plus the whole summer. So I moved back home and got a job waiting tables at night. I worked six days a week, as many hours as they would give me, socking my money away for senior Jan Plan. Sometime during this period, my father asked me the second pivotal question that framed my college career:

"What are you going to do when you graduate?"

Where did this man learn to ask such diabolical questions?

WHAT I LEARNED ALONG THE WAY

College was a critical time and place for me. It was where I first began to synthesize some key principles that have guided my life ever since.

DO WHAT YOU LOVE AND ...

London was my first real-life experience with the concept, "Do what you love, and the money will follow." Busking turned out to be unexpectedly lucrative.

If I'd told anyone that I planned to earn a respectable income in London by singing in the subway, they would have told me, "Sure thing, Charlie." But from the moment I heard my first subway busker, I knew this was something I *had* to try. The appeal was obvious: I could do something I love, flirt with beautiful British women, make my own hours, and be an active part of the London scene. The income potential was not so obvious, at least at the outset. But from the moment I strummed my first G chord at the South Kensington stop, I was averaging about twenty bucks an hour—a C-note for a five-hour "shift." All tax free.

I had friends who had to work forty hours a week to earn that kind of money.

The record-store gig was the same kind of thing. I fell into it because I loved music, but it ended up supporting my lifestyle beautifully in its own organic way.

We all have unique gifts, and the universe wants us to do what we are designed to do. When we do that thing, the universe eventually sees to it that we make a pretty good living.

It's all about energy. It comes down to that river again, that current of life. Doing what you love is a *downstream* activity. When you follow the direction you naturally want to go in, you harness the current. You use energy much more efficiently. Forcing yourself to do something you don't love, on the other hand, is an *upstream* activity. You row against the current. You create friction. Most of the energy you expend is canceled out.

In short: doing what you love *gives* you energy; doing what you hate *costs* you energy. In college I was able to function as an honors economics student, with all its rigorous demands (such as writing a 170-page paper that rivaled a PhD dissertation), while also living full-time in the theater. How? Because both of these activities were feeding me energy on some level.

Of course, I still needed to rest from time to time. But something I began to notice in college was that there is a difference between "good exhaustion" and "bad exhaustion." When you are doing what you love, you may get exhausted, yes, but it's a good, "I left every-thing on the playing field" kind of exhaustion. You go to sleep feeling tired but fulfilled. "Bad" exhaustion results from doing things that go against your grain. You feel drained, emptied, depleted.

In college I learned that I never want to feel that way.

THE HEART AND THE BRAIN BOTH NEED A SAY

Another important principle I learned in college—though I may not have been consciously aware of it at the time—is that both the heart and the brain are essential to managing a life.

We humans are unique creatures. We have two sources of intel-ligence within us: the intelligence of the heart and the intelligence of the brain. Both are vital. We ignore either one at our own peril.

The two distinct tracks my life had been running on, practically since birth—finance and acting—became *starkly* distinct in college. My brain was pulling me toward the financial side of life; my heart was pulling me toward the theater. (It wasn't that simple, of course, but you get the idea.) In college I had not yet figured out a way to synthesize these two passions, but I felt a strong need to keep my trains running on both of these tracks.

Listening to both my heart and head was vital—and I think it is for everyone. It was my heart that coaxed me to sing in the London subway and spend every night in the theater. But it was my brain that stopped me from making the catastrophic decision to stay in London and manage a jazz store instead of finishing college. I'm glad I listened to both.

In my work I meet many people who listen only to their brains. They're the ones who trade their dreams for a paycheck and patiently wait out retirement, never doing what they love. But I've also met many people—in theater and elsewhere—who listen only to their "softer," more intuitive side. They "follow their bliss" right off a cliff. These people are always broke or in one life crisis after another, because they don't listen to the voice of logic and rationality.

We need *both* sources of intelligence. Not to live life on two separate tracks—as I did for many, many years—but to bring the two into harmony. One of the great accomplishments of a human life, I think, is to learn how to put your heart and your brain into coherence with one another, so you can make decisions that simultaneously satisfy both.

I didn't know how to do that as a younger man. But at least I stayed open to both channels. And that was a lifesaver. Eventually I learned to sync the brain with the heart.

FOUR

EARLY DAYS IN BUSINESS: TELL ME I CAN'T DO IT ... *PLEASE*

My father's diabolical question hung in the air like a cloud of bug spray: *What are you going to do when you graduate?*

It hit me like a sucker punch, just as his last Big Question had. (What was I going to *major* in? Come on, Dad, what part of left field did *that* come from?)

As you'll recall, my father posed Big Question number two during that period near the end of college where I was living at his house and waiting tables to earn enough to go back to London for senior Jan Plan. In response to this question, I gave my dad an answer that was precisely as well received as my last answer had been:

"I'm going to New York to be a starving actor with all my acting friends."

My answer was so far off the radar screen of what my father was expecting to hear that it literally didn't register in his consciousness.

He repeated his question as if I simply hadn't heard him the first time. "So what are you going to do when you graduate?"

"I'm ... going to move to New York and ... try to make it as an actor ... Dad."

Tick ... tick ... tick ... went the clock on the wall. Crickets chirped. Birds tweeted. Grass grew.

"Here's an idea," my father said. "While you're living here and working nights at the restaurant, why don't you work on your economics career a bit? Why don't you make a list of successful business owners and professionals here in town? Then call everyone on the list and offer to take them to lunch and find out what made them so successful?"

It was a good idea, damn him.

"Here," said Dad, hiding his Wile E. Coyote smile, "let me help you make that list."

A LIFE-CHANGING ENCOUNTER

With my dad's help, I made a list of about ten people he knew, and I did what he suggested: I called them on the phone.

Most of the people I called were quite gracious in accepting my invitation to pick their brains. One of them was a man by the name of Hillard Aronson. He was a successful financial advisor in town and a top agent for MassMutual. Meeting Hillard Aronson would change my life.

Aronson was the consummate professional and a model of success to my eager young mind. Everything he did, from the way he dressed and spoke to the way he organized his life and business, exuded the utmost integrity, flair, and attention to detail. He was a master storyteller and showman. From the moment we met, I wanted to *become* him.

During our first lunch together, he asked me the same question my father had asked about my future plans, and I gave him the same answer: I intended to be an actor in New York, blah, blah.

Aronson chuckled lightly. "Isn't that nice, young man?" A ringing endorsement if ever I heard one. He went on to ask me what I was currently doing with my life, and I told him about my evening gig in the food service industry.

"Why don't you come work for me during the day," he suggested, "and I'll teach you the guts of the life insurance business?"

Life insurance. Every young man's dream, right? *Hey kid, wanna be an astronaut?* No, thanks. *How 'bout a movie star?* Nah. *Cowboy? Rock star? World explorer?* No, no, and no. *Have you ever considered getting into the life insurance game? Now* you're talking!

But the fact was I *wasn't* doing anything during the day, and I loved making money. And I desperately wanted to make enough to go back to London. So, if he was going to pay me money to learn something I didn't know, hey why not?

I said yes. Thanks to my economics and math background, I learned the guts of the insurance business easily and actually found it more interesting than I thought I would. It wasn't as thrilling as doing *Hair* on Broadway, but still. Hillard Aronson took me out on his sales calls with him, and I got to watch the master at work. The guy was amazing. As I listened to him, the value and benefits of life insurance became pretty damn compelling to me.

When I left for Colgate to finish my last semester, Hillard said, "Hey kid, I'm going to be opening up a district office. Why don't you look me up when you graduate? You can come work for me."

Sure, sure, I thought. I was still fixated on going to New York to be a starving actor.

THE BIG APPLE OR THE MEDIUM-SIZED KUMQUAT?

As graduation loomed closer, the choice became more and more real: starve as an actor or thrive as an insurance agent? Hmm.

On the one hand, there loomed New York City. The Big Apple. Times Square. Broadway. "If I can make it there, I'll make it anywhere!" The City That Never Sleeps. On the other, there was Springfield, Mass. The City That Is Very Well Rested.

I crunched the numbers. I learned that 95 percent of all professional actors are unemployed. Awesome. But I also learned that 90 percent of all insurance salesmen fail in their first year.

Great. For that first year, then, I was looking at a 90 percent failure rate versus 95 percent. I figured life insurance gave me a 5 percent differential. My sweet spot, maybe?

Sadly for the romantics reading this, I did not go to New York and rent a broom closet in SoHo with all my theater friends. Instead, I moved back to the booming metropolis of Springfield, Massachusetts, put on a suit, and had *no* friends. I went to work for Hillard Aronson and MassMutual.

And instead of starving as an actor … I starved as a life insurance salesman.

THE WORST OF BOTH WORLDS

Here's how the tradeoff is supposed to work. If you pursue your passions—acting, music, art, writing, whatever—you gain the excitement and soul satisfaction of doing what you love, *but* you have to live on coffee and ramen noodles for a long time. If you forgo the passion and put on the suit and tie, you lose the excitement and soul satisfaction, *but* you gain the comfy lifestyle. I got the worst of both worlds. No passion *and* no money.

I was twenty-one, fresh out of college, living with my parents, single, alone, and miserable. I had no friends—all my college friends had either gone to New York to be starving actors or had taken jobs with Exxon Mobil, IBM, or Xerox. They were all making salaries in the high teens/low twenties to start, which in 1979 was pretty good, or living romantic bohemian lives in Greenwich Village. I was in Springfield, Massachusetts, and living on commissions—which, in those early days, were strictly theoretical.

For my first three years in the life insurance business, I was in pure survival mode. The first six months were really awful. I made so little, I *owed* people money.

My main goal—the thing all agents wanted—was to get a long-term contract with an insurer. Back in the day, MassMutual would give you a career contract and a finance agreement that paid you a monthly stipend as a draw against the commissions you earned. That meant, for me, a whopping $800 a month, which was less than $10,000 a year (even back in 1979, this was garbage money). Anything you earned over the $800, you could either draw down or let build up. But to get that prized financing contract, you had to take an aptitude test.

I am proud to say that I set a record on the MassMutual aptitude test, one that still stands to this day—and this is in a company that has been around since 1850. I scored a two. Not a two out of three, not a two out of ten, but a two out of one hundred. The lowest score ever registered in MassMutual history.

No contract for Charlie Epstein.

But a couple of people still saw something in me they wanted to believe in. The general agent at the time, John Mann, told me, "If you can do $14,000 in commissions in six months' time, I will give you that financing contract."

Hillard Aronson—who carried me during the first six months and had a ridiculous amount of confidence in me—took the challenge even further. He told me I had to make the Million Dollar Round Table my first year in business. This is an achievement 99 percent of industry professionals don't achieve *ever*, let alone in their first year in business.

I ranted to anyone who'd listen about how impossible this goal was. But then one day my brother said to me, "Why don't you prove Hillard *right*? Instead of proving his faith in you is unwarranted, which will just cement your notion that you're not good enough, why don't you do everything in your power to *make* the Million Dollar Round Table?"

It was a mind-altering new way of approaching life.

LESSONS FROM THE LIFE INSURANCE TRADE

I buckled down and decided to beat the odds.

MassMutual wasn't much help in that regard. Its approach was to give you two weeks of training and throw you out on the street, saying, "There's 200 million people out there—go get 'em, tiger!" Starting out they gave you a sheet where you had to fill in a hundred names of potential people you could sell to. I managed to fill in *four*: my mother, father, sister, and brother. After that my prospects ran out.

So it was cold calling from day one: "Hi, my name's Charlie Epstein. I'm affiliated with MassMut—" *Click*. Over and over. And remember, this was 1979. There were no cell phones and no personal computers. Everything we did was with a rotary phone, a pencil, a calculator, and a yellow pad.

But I was armed with the knowledge I had learned from Hillard about the true value of life insurance and a burning desire to succeed.

I was relentless, and I had thick skin. And I was creative. Potent combo.

AN EARLY SUCCESS THAT INSPIRED

Back then the mantra for cold callers was ten-three-one. If you made ten calls, you would book three appointments and make one sale. I bought into it. In my mind if I just made more calls than anyone else on the planet, I would book more appointments and make more sales.

At the time, I noticed a large number of young people were moving back to the Springfield area to work in family businesses and professional jobs. Many of them were moving into a new apartment complex downtown. The original Milton Bradley toy factory had been converted into upscale apartments with high ceilings, brick walls, and wood beams. A yuppy paradise.

So, I went over and copied the names of all 116 residents from the labels on the entry buzzers. And back then, when you called 411, you got a live operator, and you could ask for up to five numbers at a time. By calling 411 over and over, I got the numbers for all 116 people who lived in that complex. And every Sunday evening, after 6:30 p.m., I would "dial for dollars" and cold call everyone who lived there.

I remember this one exchange that served as an inspiration to me. I called this gentleman—I still remember his name: David Wenning—at 7:15 on a Sunday and launched into my spiel.

"Hi, my name is Charlie Epstein, and I'm affiliated with the MassMutual life insur—"

He interrupted me, screaming, "Don't you ever, ever call me on a Sunday night at home!" along with a few other choice phrases.

Now, most people would have just hung up the phone, embarrassed, but I had a quota to meet. So I calmly responded, "Where should I call you?"

David thundered, "At work!"

"I'd love to call you at work," I said, "but I don't have your number."

David bellowed his work number into the phone, and I scribbled it on my yellow pad. "What would be a good time to call you?" I asked, all sweetness and joy.

"Call me at 8:30 a.m.!" he screamed and hung up.

The following morning, at eight thirty on the dot, I was on the horn to David Wenning. "Hi, this is Charlie Epstein with MassMutual Life Insurance. You asked me to call you at eight thirty."

David responded, in a surprisingly meek voice, "Charlie, I'm so sorry I was such an a-hole last night. I really do need to meet with you. See, I'm getting married next month, and I need life insurance." We met, and he purchased the life insurance policy that provided him and his future family the greatest benefit.

Ten-three-one, baby, ten-three-one.

THE BAYSTATE EMERGENCY ROOM CAPER

In those early days, Hillard, my mentor, was smart enough to pair me with another "starving young agent" by the name of Ron Sussman. Unlike me, Ron was married and had a young baby, so his need to succeed was even more pressing than mine.

Three evenings a week, Ron and I would sit in our adjacent offices religiously making our ten-three-one calls, hundreds of them a week, to make our sales quota.

One day Hillard suggested we should start calling on the young MD residents at our local hospital, Baystate Medical Center. Hillard's own financial practice was made up primarily of successful doctors. He said, "If you provide value to these interns while they're young and struggling—like you are—then later, when they go into private practice and their incomes skyrocket, they'll look to you to continue to furnish them with products and services."

Made sense. But how to get to these young MDs in training who were working 120 hours a week?

I remembered that the hospital posted the names and pictures of the current crop of residents on a huge sheet behind the nurses' station at the ER entrance. I said to Ron, "If we could get hold of that sheet, we would have all the residents' names, and we could call information and get their numbers."

"How are we going to do that?" inquired Ron.

Ever the actor, I had the script ready.

One evening around midnight, Ron and I drove up to the entrance of Baystate's emergency room. I entered the sliding doors first; Ron lurked in the shadows behind me. I strolled up to the desk and asked the night nurse for the name of a fictitious patient. As she was looking up the name, I began to groan and sway in front of her.

"Sir, are you all right?" she asked, alarmed.

"Actually, I'm feeling a bit nauseous and dizzy," I rasped. And then I collapsed to the floor, right in front of her counter. She, of course, came rushing from behind the desk to attend to me. Ron took his cue. Springing from the shadows, he dashed behind the nurses' desk, ripped the interns' photo sheet from the wall, and darted out the side entrance.

When he was safely out the door, I sat up, looked at the night nurse, kissed her on the cheek, and said, "Wow, I feel so much better now. Thank you for your help." Then I stood up and slipped out the exit into Ron's getaway car. And off into the night we roared, cackling like two kids who had just robbed a bank in broad daylight.

The next day we were on the phone with every intern on that sheet, scheduling appointments to review their current benefits packages and insure their families' financial future.

LESSON FROM A BMW

It was tough in those early years, surviving on those monthly draws of $800. I remember living in the second-floor apartment of a two-family house on Hamburg Street with my girlfriend (later my wife), Ellen—whom I'll talk about later. She was a bartender living on tips, and I was living from stipend payment to stipend payment. Floating our rent checks was a painfully regular experience for us.

But I did own a BMW 320i. Really? How? And why?

First, the how. My dead grandfather provided the means. Max Epstein, you see, had purchased an overfunded $5,000 whole-life policy for each of his twelve grandchildren when we were born. So I borrowed the cash value from that policy and used it to buy a beautiful, used white BMW 320i.

Why? I figured if I *looked* successful, then the clients I was calling on, who were usually much older than me, wouldn't view me as a poor, struggling life insurance agent. Which I was. They would view me as a success.

The first winter I owned that car, we had one of the worst blizzards in the history of western Mass. The walls of our apartment were so thin and uninsulated you could feel each blast of arctic air rippling through our apartment. Ellen and I couldn't afford our oil bill, and we ran out of fuel in the middle of that blizzard. We were so cold we would run downstairs to our Korean landlady's first-floor apartment every couple of hours and stand in her kitchen asking her made-up questions just to get warm.

But the genius of buying that car, rather than oil for our apartment, did reveal itself a couple of months later.

I was in a finalist meeting with a guy named Butchie, the owner of a construction company. I had just finished making a presentation on why he should buy life insurance for him and his partner to fund a buy-sell agreement in the event one of them passed away.

Butchie looked at his partner and said, "So we have to decide who to buy this life insurance from. Do we buy it from the guy who works for Mutual of New York and drives a pickup truck, or do we buy it from the guy who works for MassMutual and drives a BMW 320i?"

"What's your decision?" I inquired.

He smiled at me and said, "The guy driving the BMW 320i of course." And we both laughed as he and his partner signed the application.

It was a life lesson. You have to spend money to make money. To this day I have never stopped investing in myself, my employees, my business, and my bigger future.

. . .

At the end of my first year in business, Ron Sussman and I shared the Young Agent of the Year award, and I made the Million Dollar Round Table (MDRT), a feat achieved by only the top 1 percent of all life insurance professionals. I was twenty-two years old and had proven at least one thing beyond a reasonable doubt: MassMutual's aptitude test needed major revamping!

Qualifying for the MDRT offered me the amazing opportunity to attend my first MDRT conference at Radio City Music Hall in the Big Apple. It was four days of mixing with successful colleagues and listening to great inspirational speakers. Two of those speakers would impact my life in ways only time would allow me to truly embrace.

The first, Marshall Wooper of Miami, Florida, would change my understanding of money and leverage. He shared how he borrowed $1 million to start his pension business in the 1960s. He said he felt he had "no choice" but to succeed, because he had to pay that money back.

I wrote on my hand. "Borrow … million dollars … Invest In Self."

The second, Ray Triplett, would change my understanding of time.

Ray shared how he had made more money by working less. He did it by fulfilling his boyhood dream of sailing around the world. It took him five years. He and his wife would get in their thirty-seven-foot sailboat and sail for nine months, and then he would return home for three months to work in his business. He made more money working for three months than he had made working year-round!

I wrote on my hand, "Work three months, make more money, while doing what you love for the other nine months."

I will be forever indebted to both Marshall and Ray for what they taught me!

I would go on to become Agent of the Year seven years in a row. I would also become one of the top ten most successful agents out of 5,600 in the MassMutual nation and a member of the Top of the Table, the top 500 life insurance agents in the world in terms of income.

For my first three years of my life insurance career, I lived only on that $800 monthly draw, so at the end of my first three-year contract, I got a check for almost $20,000, which was a nice year's salary back then. I had also netted my first set of long-term clients, and, most of all, I had learned the law of "No doesn't mean never; it just means not now."

Some other important things happened during those early adult years. I met and moved in with Ellen, the woman who would become my first wife. (The fact that I use the term "my *first* wife" offers a hint at how things turned out there.) I also got involved with *est*. For those of you not familiar with est—always spelled in lowercase letters— it stood for Erhard Seminars Training. It was an intense "transfor- mational" self-development program created by Werner Erhard of Landmark Forum fame. My involvement with est opened the door for later spiritual adventures and transformations. Both my marriage and est were extremely important facets of my life, but I will talk about them later.

The next thing I want to share with you is how my love of acting worked its way back into my life. But first ...

WHAT I LEARNED ALONG THE WAY

My postcollege years were rich with lessons I have built a career upon ...

"NO" NEVER MEANS NEVER; IT JUST MEANS NOT NOW

The greatest thing selling insurance and making cold calls taught me was that *no never means never; it just means not now.* Understanding this principle has opened more doors than any other principle I've ever learned.

No is a temporary thing, not a permanent state. The first time a person hears an idea, their reflexive reaction is almost always to say *no*. It doesn't mean, "I hate this idea, and I'll never consider it"; it just means, "This is a new idea, and I'm going to have to get used to it before I say yes." It's your job, as the seller, the proposer, the architect of the idea, to continue presenting your idea until the other person gets comfortable with it and becomes persuaded. Decision-making is a slow process for most people, and it involves the emotions as well as the head. Getting to yes takes time.

There's an old saw in sales that it takes seven noes to get to a yes. Some say it's *ten* noes. The number doesn't matter. The point is that noes are part of the process of getting to yes.

Think about yourself. Do you immediately say yes to a new idea, even if it seems like a good one? You do not. You say no, and then you go home and think about it. No is a multipurpose word. It can mean *I'm not sure; I don't feel like dealing with this right now; I need more information; convince me more; I need to talk to someone else; I need to do some online research;* and a thousand other things.

We all *say* no to mean any and all of these things, but when we *hear* a no, we treat it as a closed door. We take no as a final answer. Even worse, we see it as a rejection. We hear a "you're not good enough" in the no.

But think of dogs. When a doorbell rings, what do dogs do? They run to the door. Is the door ever for them? Never. Do they go sulk in a corner, hating themselves? Nope, they just shrug it off. "Maybe next time it'll be for me." And the next time the bell rings, they run to the door again for yet another no. The difference between a dog and a human is … a dog never takes it personally.

But people do. Most of us stop at the first no and never come back.

Me, I'm all about the noes. Bring 'em on. I try to get to *no* as quickly as possible. Because it means I'm that much closer to getting to the treasured yes.

During that period when I was making those cold calls on cold Sunday evenings, my mentor Hillard Aronson told me, "Kid, before you pick up that phone, put a smile on your face and say out loud, 'Who's going to be lucky enough to talk to me tonight?' And then start dialing."

Try it!

MOCK IT UP TILL YOU MAKE IT

You've probably heard the expression, "Fake it till you make it." I agree with its sentiment, but I don't like the "fake it" part. It implies falseness, pretense, insincerity. There's nothing fake about behaving *as if* you have already achieved the goals you are striving for. In fact that's the secret to manifesting one's desires—as taught by countless spiritual masters throughout time.

We human beings are resistant to change. Our habit is always to shrink back into the familiar molds into which we have poured our lives. The best way to facilitate change is to behave *as if* the change has already taken place. This starts the process of stretching the molds, making them bigger, so that our lives can flow into them. Want to move to a different socioeconomic level? Start dressing, talking, and acting the part. Want to own a bigger home? Start hanging around bigger homes and breathing the air in bigger homes. Want to become a successful writer? Start acting and speaking like a successful writer. Stretch the mold.

It's not fakery; it's authenticity. It's being true to the goals of your heart. When we behave *as if* we already have the things we desire, we retrain our habits and emotions. We become comfortable seeing ourselves in a new way. And then the actual success becomes all but inevitable. We've already changed the mold.

LIMITATIONS CAN BE A PRISON CELL OR A SPRINGBOARD

I love it when someone tells me I can't do something. I take it as a challenge, and a welcome one. It gives me something to push off from.

When I was younger, I had that rebellious, oppositional nature I've described in detail. When you told me I couldn't do something, I said, in effect, "Oh yeah? Well, I'll show *you*." These days I don't have that chip on my shoulder anymore. I don't really care about proving anyone wrong. It's not about other people anymore. But I do still get value from having my limitations challenged. I still use it as a springboard for growth.

Here's something I've realized. If someone points out a limitation in me and it irks me in some way, that's because there's part of me that believes it. It has nothing to do with the other person; it's a belief I have about myself. And now I need to work at going beyond it.

From the time we're born, other people begin boxing us in and defining us, in ways that are convenient to *them*, not us. By the time we're in school, we've reduced ourselves to a fraction of our natural capacity and developed the habit of letting others define us. A great way to escape this trap is to take limitations as a challenge.

Think of President John F. Kennedy in 1961 standing up and telling the nation, "We will put a man on the moon by the end of the decade." He had no idea how to make that statement a reality. But having made that commitment—and having the Soviet Union to compete against—gave us a springboard to greatness. It drove us to be better as a nation.

What are some limitations you can start challenging today?

How many "noes" have you been stopping at?

What roadblocks does your mind concoct every day to rob you of your bigger future?

When will you pick up the phone, look in the mirror and say, "Who's going to be lucky enough to talk with me today?" Your bigger, brighter, more amazing future is only a dial tone and seven noes away!

My grandfather on my dad's side, Max Epstein: the Entrepreneur/CPA.
He always had a cigar in one hand, a cup of black coffee in the other, amid a big
smile on his face, like he knew the secret. I always wanted to know the secret.

My grandfather on my mom's side, Henry E. Burtaine: The Entertainer/Artist.
He was concertmaster of radio city in the 1920's and a starving artist/painter.

Where it all began… The Bride and Groom celebrate
their wedding day April 16, 1950.

My mother, the Opera Singer. She studied at Julliard in
NYC and the Hart School of Music in Conneticut. Here
she is as the Witch in the opera *Hansel and Gretel*.

And backstage (second to left) with her fellow performers.
Note the cigarette and drink in everyone's hands!

My dad served in World War II and the Korean War as a Lieutenant in the Army. Seen below with his Dad, Max, just before he got deployed to Burma.

"Baby go baba car mom..." Suiting up with the siblings, my sister Deborah, and my brother, Paul (right), circa 1965.

Four years old, waiting for my "big break" on the doorstep of my first house on East Allen Ridge Road, Springfield, MA.

First signs of talent at nine years old, doing impersonations around
the house for my mother. "Say the Secret Word" … Groucho

My first big lead Junior year in high school as Harold Hill…
The Music Man. I had two different leading ladies to contend with.

Top: The Athlete — Lacrosse, Sophomore Year, Hich School (1973)

Bottom left: The Editor — Longmeadow High School Jet Jotter (1975)

Bottom right: The Saxophonist, aka Chuck "The Clam"
— Longmeadow High School (1972-1975)

Taking on leading roles in college at Colgate University,
1975-1979, here as "The Devil" in *Damn Yankees*.

And the Evil Jonathan Brewster in the classic *Arsenic and Old Lace*. Boris Karloff originated the role on Broadway.

Studying in London, 1977, at the London School of Economics. My real economic education was "street busking" in the subways of London. I was making "10 Quid" an hour which was equivalent to $17 US in 1977!

Hanging with my crazy roommates Mark, Pete, me, and Rick in our London flat with some unknown blonde. We had a pub across the street where we did most of our studying… and drinking warm beer by the pints!

My father's now famous response when I told him I was going to be a theatre major at Colgate University, "Yeah, that and ten cents will get you a cup of coffee." My immediate response, "I'll be an economics major and live in the theater." He approved and the rest is history.

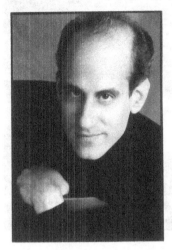

Charles Burtaine

AEA • SAG

212-501-2474

Somebody please hire this "starving" actor.

Summer 1988. After eight years building my financial business, I got a job as a summer intern at Monmouth Theatre, the state's Shakespearean Theatre, in Monmouth, Maine. I'm thirty-one years old getting paid $27.75 a week PLUS room and board. Give an actor a place to perform and we will work for free! Here I am playing the Duke of York in Richard II.

6-17-88	Charles D. Epstein		30	2.25					27 75
PERIOD ENDING	EMPLOYEE'S NAME	HRS.	GROSS PAY	FICA	I. TAX	ST. TAX	P.R.S.		NET PAY

PLEASE DETACH — RETAIN FOR YOUR RECORDS
THE THEATER AT MONMOUTH — MONMOUTH, MAINE 04259

The Theater At Monmouth
Cumston Hall   Monmouth, Maine · 04259

REMITTANCE ADVICE

52-24/112

Nº   492

PAY AMOUNT   Twenty — seven and 75/100   Dollars

DATE   TO THE ORDER OF   PAYMENT FOR   CHECK AMOUNT
6-17-88   Charles D. Epstein   W/e: 6-17-88   27 75

THE THEATER AT MONMOUTH

Kim Gordon

NORSTAR BANK — MONMOUTH, MAINE

⑆000492⑆ ⑆011200242⑆ 00 685 404 4⑆

My first official paycheck as an actor! (Don't give up that day job!!)

Some of the many fun roles I've enjoyed performing over the years:

Top: One of the "Crazy" neighbors in *The Odd Couple*, Mt. Holyoke
Summer Theater, 1993. Bottom left: *Tomfoolery* a musical revival based
on the songs of Tom Lehrer. I got to sing the Chemical Elements Table to
the music of *Modern Major General*, from *The Pirates of Penzance*. Bottom
right: Amos in *All that Jazz*, Block Island Summer Theatre, 1992.

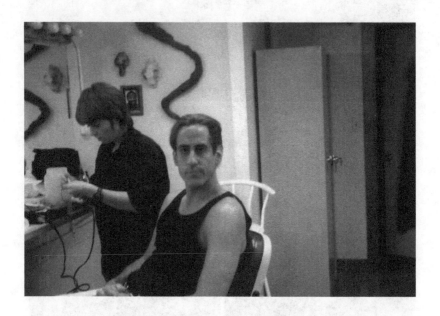

My tour de force, *Solitary Confinement*, by Rupert Holmes. He had won three Tony Awards for *The Secret of Edwin Drood*. I got to play all seven roles. The makeup took three hours for each character. Rupert drove up from NYC to see the last performance with his ninety-two year old mother. After the show he said, "This role and this show is yours to perform anywhere you choose!"

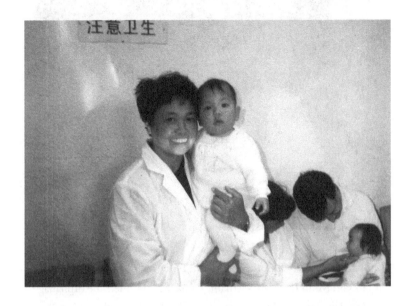

Adopting my daughter Hannah (Wu Ming Bo) in Kunming, China, 1995

First time visiting my son Noah (Chin Dinh Phan) in his Orphanage in Ho Chi Minh (Saigon) Vietnam, January 2022. I left the orphanage that day and cycled for two weeks from Ho Chi Minh to Hanoi.

Me, on my two-week cycling trip from Ho Chi Minh to Hanoi. Taking a "water" break pit stop along the way.

Sister Hannah (age five) first time meeting and holding her new brother, Noah, in the orphanage in Ho Chi Minh, Vietnam, March 2022.

Raising Sheep on my "gentleman farm" in Somer, CT. Learning how to shear them and hanging with my sheep dog, Powder, and Sam the Ram.

My first encounter with Swami Kaleshwar, Austin, Texas, May 22, 2006

I was in the middle of my "horrific" divorce and feeling like the
character Kevin Costner played in the movie *No Way Out*. I asked
Swami that day for just one wish... and within twenty-four hours,
he provided it for me. I will forever be indebted to him.

WITH CHARLIE EPSTEIN

JUNE 23, 24 AND 25 AT 7:30 P.M.
Leslie Phillips Theatre | Holyoke Community College
303 Homestead Avenue, Holyoke

Yield of Dreams Original Creative Team: Ryan Hicks, Jesse Egan, Charlie Epstein, Mike Koenigs, Marissa Brassfield (not pictured: Kyle Ray)

After a year of writing, rehearsing, and tweaking, we opened the original version of *Yield of Dreams* August 2021 at The Northampton Arts Center to rave reviews. June of 2022 saw the revised version of *Yield of Dreams* at HCC College, Holyoke, MA. These performances have inspired me to work on a fifty College Campus tour in 2024 and beyond. Stay tuned!

The secret to a great life—great friends. From left to right, my friends
of forty-five years, Joel, Roy, me, David, Barry, and Mark.

Hannah and Noah all grown up.

My "Hero," Biggest Fan (oh, and critic, too!), and Business Partner, Lorie, my wife. God put a "slow hit" on me the day she backed her Jeep into me. We work together, yell and laugh, and travel the globe together.

Top: My extended family — The Bemis Clan. My wife Lorie's
daughter, Kim, grandson Riley (19), graduating high school, Dad,
Major Carl Bemis, and grandsons, Brady (15) and Ryan (17)

Bottom: My two amazing step-children- Kim Bemis, who was
a Helicopter Medic in the Air Force and Marc Chapdelaine, a
Technical Sergeant currently serving in the Air Force.

Celebrating ten years of wedded bliss
at Amanyara, Turks & Caicos, August 8, 2020

FIVE

A RETURN TO THEATER: LEARNING HOW TO BEND TIME

Life insurance is a fascinating thing. No joke. When I was younger, I thought of it as just a way to provide your loved ones with a pile of cash when you croak. But as I started selling it, I began to learn what a versatile and powerful financial tool it can be. Because of tax rules and other regulations, a whole-life policy or indexed universal life policy can be used in unique ways to build and protect wealth. It should be part of every thinking person's wealth portfolio. Don't even get me started.

The more I worked with life insurance, and talked to clients about it, the more I began to realize it was no accident that Hillard Aronson was both a life insurance agent and a financial advisor. It was natural, when talking to clients about their life insurance needs, to look at their whole financial picture. And to talk to them about their life goals, their hopes and dreams, their families, and their legacies. Like Hillard, I began to transition into financial advising.

Eventually, financial advising became my chief focus, and selling life insurance became an adjunct to that. I built my own successful financial service firm; a registered investment advisory firm, Epstein Financial Services; a successful benefits company; a community bank; and a thriving family business center at the University of Massachusetts that survived the odds for twenty-five years! My focus, in all my financial advising work, was to help people create self-generating income—paychecks for life—so that they could create the time and freedom in their lives to pursue what they desired most in life. I even coined a word to transform how my industry talks about financial planning: desirement (as opposed to retirement). Go ahead—google "desirement" and see what pops up.

But what about *my* true dreams? What about *my* life passion of becoming a successful working actor? Had I put it out to pasture forever?

A CATTLE CALL GETS THE BALL ROLLING

After eight years of *talking* about acting, *pining* for acting, and "shoulda-woulda-coulda-ing" my decision to pursue finance, I saw a notice in the paper for the annual NETC theater auditions. The New England Theater Conference was an organization dedicated to advancing the theater arts in New England. Every year it held a huge, open "cattle call" for all the summer theaters in the northeast states. The event lasted for three days and was always held at the auditorium of a Boston-area college/university, such as Brandeis or Tufts. Directors and producers from all over New England would attend, shopping for talented, nonunion actors to fill out the casts of their summer productions. And hundreds, maybe thousands, of actors—

professional and otherwise—would show up to parade their talents. Or lack thereof.

I'd known about the infamous NETC auditions for years but had never participated. In March of 1987, though, I said a hearty f*ck it, jumped in my car, and drove the two hours to Tufts University in Medford, Massachusetts, just outside of Boston.

The NETC cattle call had one simple rule. You got two minutes on stage to do your prepared audition, not a millisecond more. They called it a cattle call for a reason. Can I get a moo?

Now, you have to remember that even though I'd been pretty successful as a college actor, I hadn't set foot on a stage since 1979. Nervous as a Kardashian facing a PhD committee, I walked out onto that stage and did my two-minute memorized piece. Before I even finished, some guy in the wings with a stopwatch yelled, "Thank you. Next!"

I shuffled off the stage and went to a coffee joint to kill a few hours while I waited for them to post the callback sheet at the end of the day. Unable to stay away, though, I returned to the Tufts theater and paced like an expectant father until the staff announced that the callback sheet had been posted. I rushed to see it.

Not one theater hired me or even requested me to do a callback audition. I couldn't even get anyone to let me pay *them* to be an intern for the summer!

I think the reason I went back into acting was that I wasn't getting enough rejection selling life insurance. "Thank you ... Next!"

OUT OF THE BLUE A FATEFUL LETTER ARRIVES

I was heartbroken as I drove the two hours back from Boston to Springfield, *"Thank you. Next!"* still ringing in my ears. I figured my fate was sealed; I was going to be a financial professional for the rest of my life and, like my mother the opera singer, was never going to fulfill my true calling of being a successful performer.

"Thank you. Next."

"Thank you. Next."

"Thank you. Next."

Then, something magical happened. A month later, out of the clear blue, I received a letter in the mail—an invitation—to study Shakespeare for a month at the University of Connecticut, with the Royal Academy of Dramatic Arts (RADA).

To this day I have no idea how, in that preinternet era, they got hold of my name or why I received this invitation. My guess is that someone saw me at the cattle call and thought I showed promise. Or money. I'll never know. And it didn't matter. I took it as a *sign*.

I enrolled. I took the entire month of July 1987 off, and for thirty days I immersed myself in everything Shakespeare—Shakespearean diction, Shakespearean movement, Shakespearean text interpretation, Shakespearean sonnets, even Shakespearean clowning. I took fight classes from three of the most talented English Shakespearean teachers on the planet. The course ran six days a week, fifteen hours a day. Intense. And I'd never been so inspired in my life. I wanted it to last a year.

CATTLE CALL NUMBER TWO

Best of all, at the end of that magical month, I had crafted a new two-minute audition for the 1988 cattle call. For the next eight months, I rehearsed that two-minute audition in the rearview mirror of my car and in the halls and bathrooms of my home (much to the delight of my wife, who celebrated by buying a Sony Walkman and never taking the earphones off).

The acoustics in the bathroom were the best. I still remember that soliloquy verbatim:

> *Now is the winter of our discontent*
> *Made glorious summer by this sun of York;*
> *And all the clouds that lour'd upon our house*
> *In the deep bosom of the ocean buried.*
> *Now are our brows bound with victorious wreaths;*
> *Our bruised arms hung up for monuments;*
> *Our stern alarms changed to merry meetings,*
> *Our dreadful marches to delightful measures …*

In the spring of 1988, I drove back to that open call in Boston and strode confidently back on stage in front of those hundreds of directors who had unanimously rejected me the year before. Only this time I delivered my flawless and perfectly timed two-minute audition and then walked off without a look back. If I'd been using a mic, I would have dropped it.

At the end of the day, I waited for the gathered crowd of thespian hopefuls to disperse, then read the oversized callback sheet posted on the bulletin board.

They liked me—they really liked me! A theater had offered me a job—the States Shakespearean Theater in Monmouth, Maine. Dick Sewell, the director and head of theater studies at Colby College, was offering to *pay me* an actual salary, plus room and board, to be an intern for the entire summer.

And what was the King Richardly salary I was to receive? Twenty-five bucks a week. Yee-haw.

Hey, give an actor food and a place to sleep, and we'll work for free!

Now, you need to understand a few things to put this offer in its proper context. First of all, the average age of a summer theater intern was eighteen. I was thirty-one at the time. Second, the theater in Monmouth was a four-and-a-half-hour drive from my home and office, one way. Third, I would be there six days a week, working sixteen to twenty hours a day, for three full months—June, July, and August. That meant I would have just one day a week—Monday, when the theater was dark—to keep my financial advising business afloat, my bills paid, my employees paid, and my wife happy (a whole nother challenge).

And of course, there was the small matter of compensation. At the time, I was earning about $10,000 a week in my financial business, so I was about to take a 4,000 percent pay cut!

I couldn't say yes fast enough.

And thus began a twenty-year odyssey of pursuing theater and finance simultaneously.

BENDING TIME

When I reported for the first day of work in my business suit, let's just say I didn't exactly fit in. That first week, a Tony Award–winning actress showed up to guest star. She took one look at me and said, "What is *that* doing here?" And when I made up a new bit of staging during a live performance of *Richard II*, a local leading actress was so furious, she throttled me off stage, then threw me back on stage, right on cue! Timing is everything in live theater.

To say I was a blithering idiot as an actor would be an insult to blithering idiots. But I loved it and kept at it. During those three months in Monmouth, I did every type of theater job imaginable, from building sets to sewing costumes. The director took notice, and I got to play an old footman and an outlaw in *Twelfth Night*, the Duke of York in *Richard II*, and Hark the Spy in the children's play.

Sunday nights I would drive home, arriving in the wee hours of the morning. And then, on the one day per week allotted to my financial business—Monday—I would work from 4:30 a.m. to 11:00 p.m., filling my day with enough appointments to keep the lights on and the tax man happy.

Back at Monmouth the other interns posted a sign over the pay phone backstage: "Epstein Financial Services." During our rehearsal breaks, I would sneak off and use that phone to make enough calls to fill my one day with appointments (remember, ten-three-one!). And yes, I did say *pay phone*; this was the pre–cell phone era, especially in the sticks of Monmouth, Maine. The theater even assigned an intern to get me (an intern) off the phone and back to rehearsals on time!

Sounds like a formula for stress and misery, right? It wasn't. I had never been more exhilarated, invigorated, challenged, pushed to my limits … exhausted! I was finally doing what I had always dreamed of, no more excuses. And at the end of that year, 1988, having worked only nine months in my financial business, I'd made $50,000 more than I did the year before, working all twelve months in my financial business.

How? How could I have worked less and made more money? It felt like I had discovered an amazing principle. Just like Ray Triplett, who took nine months off to go sailing, I had figured out how to bend time!

Most of us view time as a linear phenomenon: there are sixty seconds in a minute, sixty minutes in an hour, twenty-four hours in a day, seven days in a week. Time is fixed, finite, you can't change it. Logically, the more time you spend in your chosen profession, the more money you make. Yet here I was, doing the polar opposite. It felt like I was breaking the laws of physics!

But no, I was tapping into the laws of personal economics. Emotional supply and demand. The supply of time I had to work in my business had gone down 25 percent, while my expenses kept going up, so I started to value my time even more. And the more valuable something is, the less likely you are to waste it. I had to do in nine months what I used to do in twelve.

And this attitude carried over into my performing. If I only had three months to pursue the theater, then I owed it to myself to focus 100 percent of my energy on being the best actor I could be. After all, the other thirty-one-year-old actors were not interns. They were professional artists. Thirteen years ahead of me in perfecting their craft. It felt like I was never going to stack up. So I had to bend time to my demands and spend every moment I could watching and learning from them. I accelerated the process and speed of studying my craft.

Albert Einstein showed us that you can bend time. His theory of relativity introduced us to the notion of "space-time." Time isn't linear, he pointed out; it's relative to your experiences. Time flies when you're having fun, and you get more done in less time when you spend it doing what you love.

But until I stepped onto that stage at Monmouth Theater, I had no fricking clue what Einstein was talking about. But then, just like Alice in Wonderland, I fell into that rabbit hole, and life as I knew it was never the same again. The phenomenon of producing more in less time became my singular focus for the next twenty years!

Money became secondary to me; I now knew it would take care of itself. Chasing my life's passion became my new life's currency.

NEW YORK CALLS AGAIN

In 1989 Monmouth called me back to do the lead in the children's play *The Red Shoes*. I played an evil gypsy for a month—two shows a day, mornings and afternoons, six days a week. This time around I wasn't an intern, so I had time on my hands in the evenings. I started hanging around with the other actors and getting to know them a bit.

They all told me the same thing: "You should go to New York and take classes and audition."

New York. She was calling me again. This time I was going to answer the call, damn it. I got hired by a theater company in the Village to do two months of summer theater on Block Island.

And then, not long afterward, I found myself ensconced in Manhattan: subletting a room with a chair and a bed on West Fourteenth Street between Eleventh and Twelfth, taking a commercial acting class and trying my hand at stand-up comedy.

I was finally doing the starving New York actor thing—though I wasn't actually starving.

I remember coming home one night about one in the morning, jacked up from doing a good comedy set. (My apartment was in the meat market, and I knew all the sex workers on my corner by name—*Morning, Crystal! Oh, hi, Charlie.*) I walked into my little apartment and turned the TV on, and I heard this voice say, "Acting is living truthfully in imaginary circumstances."

It was as if a bolt of lightning had shot through my heart. My eyes and ears were riveted to the TV. The show was about Sandy Meisner, the famed actor and acting teacher. Meisner, along with people like Lee Strasberg and Stella Adler, had come up through the Group Theatre, where they lived and breathed Stanislavski's famous "method." He eventually broke away to create his own version of method acting known as the Meisner method. And that was the basic premise of his acting approach: learning how to live truthfully under imaginary circumstances.

I wanted in. When I got up the next morning, I started looking up every Meisner teacher in New York City. It was more than a handful, let me tell you. I think I interviewed twelve of them.

I remember this one guy who was a disciple of Meisner—flamboyant guy with a little cigarette in his mouth. At the end of the interview, he looked at me and said, "We'll decide if you're acceptable and get back to you." And I leaned across his desk—I was thirty-two at the time, remember, not one of the nineteen-year-old wannabes he was used to dealing with—and said, "I don't think you understand what's going on here. *I'm* interviewing *you*. I'll let you know if you passed my test and get back to you." And I got up and walked out.

I finally met a teacher I liked at the School for Film and Television. Her name was Mary Doyle, and her brother was the actor Tom Bosley who played the father on TV's famous *Happy Days* with "the Fonz." Tiny woman, about five feet tall, chain-smoker. I remember doing my two-minute audition for her (a requirement to get into the program), and when I was done, she just sat there with her cigarette, blowing smoke, for about twenty seconds. Then she said, rather caustically, "Oh, we have much work to do …"

I got accepted … And work I did.

I learned a lot from Mary and that two-year program. One thing that stuck with me was an acting story she shared. The class asked her, "What was the greatest moment you ever saw on stage?" She told us about being in the original cast of *Equus* on Broadway, with Richard Burton who played the lead role of the psychotherapist. At the time, Burton hadn't been on a live stage in fifteen years. He was a raging alcoholic, and his confidence was in the toilet. Opening night, there was a scene where he was on stage by himself. Mary, who played the nurse, was in the wings waiting to make her entrance. She remembered watching Burton walk to a bookshelf, and when he reached for a book, his hand started shaking wildly, from the nerves and the alcoholism. Most actors would have tried to cover this up, Mary said, but not Burton. He turned his body fully to the audience (naked and raw, we actors are fond of saying, with the belly open and vulnerable) and held his shaking hand up in front of his face. And then he held his other shaking hand up, and he just looked at both of his hands until they slowly stopped shaking. Then he turned to the bookshelf and grabbed the book.

Mary said it was the most amazing moment because Burton had infused his character with what was actually happening to himself, Burton, the man, right there in the moment. And in doing so, he revealed the inner turmoil his character was experiencing without uttering a single word to the audience. Acting ... living truthfully in imaginary circumstances. Bam—I wanted that!

A MISSED CUE LEADS TO A ROLE OF A LIFETIME

A miracle came out of doing that two-year program. In my first year, I got cast in a show back in Springfield, at Stage West, a professional theater. It was a tiny part. But that's not the miracle.

During that period, it happened that I had been in a bad car accident that had caused some muscle tissue damage. I was prescribed very strong muscle relaxation medication. One night the actor's classic nightmare happened. I blew a cue. There was a scene where my character was supposed to come out on stage and stop the leading actor and actress from fighting. I was backstage and fell asleep from the medication! I woke up and thought I had missed my entrance. So I went running out onto stage ... about two pages too early.

The leading two actors at first just stared at me with that look of ... "what the f—k are you doing here?!" They had to improvise their way through the scene, repairing my damage, which wasn't easy. After the show I was waiting backstage to apologize to the director, when the leading actress came storming in and basically ripped me a new one, yelling and screaming. I had no choice but to suck it up and take the abuse. Unbeknownst to me, the director was watching the whole scene in the wings. After the raging actress left, he put his arm around me and said, "Are you okay?"

I said, "I've never been so embarrassed in my life. That medication just knocked me out."

He said, most kindly, "Don't worry. It happens to all of us. Go home and have a good night's sleep. Tomorrow's a new day."

A year later, when I graduated from the program, this same director called me up and said, "I think I've got the perfect role for you. It's a lead role, if you're interested.

I was in awe that he even considered asking me given my faux pas.

Naturally intrigued, I showed up and did the reading. And I got the part. It was for a one-man show called *Solitary Confinement*, written by Rupert Holmes, the only playwright to win three Tony Awards on Broadway. It's the story of a Howard Hughes–like billionaire who is locked in self-imposed confinement. He doesn't allow any of his employees near him; they talk to him on a TV monitor. There's a three-hundred-pound French chef, an English woman who serves as his secretary, an accountant, a senile security guard—seven characters in total.

And here's the twist. All the characters are played by the same actor. Me. Only they're prerecorded, except for the main guy. If you do it right, the audience doesn't know until the end of the show that all the characters are played by one actor. In the lobby and in the program, there are seven different photos and bios of imaginary actors. It's really clever.

The great actor Stacy Keach originated the role off Broadway, and now it was my turn.

For the actor, of course, it's a hell of a wild ride. One day, during rehearsals, the director informed me, "We can't afford to do Hollywood-level makeup jobs. So we're just going to put some powder on your face and make you look like these six characters as best we can."

My response was, "Are you out of your fricking mind? People will know it's me."

My solution? I went to New York and found a pro makeup artist and paid her $5,000 out of my own pocket to come up to Massachusetts for a weekend and do the makeup. This woman did extraordinary work. Think Robin Williams in *Mrs. Doubtfire* or Eddie Murphy in *The Nutty Professor*. Prosthetics, the whole works. Each character's makeup took three-and-a-half hours.

Over the course of a Friday, Saturday, and Sunday, we created two characters a day, and we filmed each performance. (I think I collapsed on Monday.) The show went up, and for eight weeks, eight shows a week, I did this insane performance where I interacted with *myself* for two-and-a-half hours, to sold-out audiences. My family members used to say I had multiple personalities. Come to think of it, so did most of my teachers. Maybe they were about to be vindicated.

We pulled it off every night. The bows at the end were the best. Each character would take a bow on the TV screen, and the name Charles Burtaine (my stage name, in honor of my mother and grandfather, the real artists in the family) would appear below them. I'd be standing off stage and I could hear the audience muttering, "Oh my God. He played *everybody*." And then, of course, when I came out to take my live bow, they'd jump to their feet, and I'd get a crazy standing ovation. Never failed.

Last performance, Rupert Holmes, the playwright, came up from New York to see the show with his ninety-two-year-old mother. After the curtain he came to me and said, "This show is yours, if you want to take it on the road." At $525 a week, which was Equity wages for small theaters across the country, I declined, calculating I would be bankrupt by the time the show landed in Poughkeepsie! But it was the greatest compliment from a playwright I ever got as an actor. (Hmm, come to think of it, it was up until that time the only compliment I had received from a playwright, since every other play I had been in, the playwrights were all dead! Thank you, Shakespeare.)

BENDING TIME AND MAKING BANK

During the period from 1988 to 2001, a lot of amazing things happened for me, both as an actor and a finance professional. I was doing more and more with less and less time.

In 1991 I got my union card, Actors' Equity, and was officially recognized as a professional actor. I didn't need the money, but getting paid for your work as an actor is a terrific feeling.

In 1993 I got a commercial agent—Don Buchwald & Associates, Howard Stern's agency—and began auditioning every week for commercials. It took me sixty auditions to book my first commercial, but I finally got one, playing a nondescript computer geek in a CSW commercial. Most actors did it for the money; I did it for the challenge, the experience.

I played Pop in the *Popular Mechanics* video series; I landed a part on the soap opera *Guiding Light*; I got to do improv with Chicago City Limits in Manhattan; and I did stand-up with the likes of John Stewart and Caroline Rhea at Standup New York on Seventy-Sixth and Broadway.

But here was the coolest part: every time I finished a show or a class and went back to my financial practice, I was rejuvenated and singularly focused on doing my best for my clients.

I had eradicated excuse-making and stumbled on one of the secrets of life: work your passion, prune away the nonsense, and watch your life blossom before your eyes.

I did whatever it took to continue to grow my business so it would support my acting "habit." And then, when I would successfully meet my business goals, I would go back to auditioning, rehearsing, and performing, always trying to improve my craft. My financial business was the patron of my acting career.

Each year the more time I took off from my business, the more money I made than the year before. At one point my wife said, "You know, if you just stopped working altogether, we'd be millionaires!" (And then she divorced me ... and I *made* her one! Ba-dum.)

ACTING ENDS ON 9/11

By the turn of the millennium, I was regularly taking three to five months a year off from my financial business to pursue my acting career. But then something changed. In 2001 I got a call from the producer who had cast me on *Guiding Light*. He said, "I'm going to be directing this off off-Broadway show. And there's a part in it for you if you're interested."

My reaction was, "God, yes. Finally." With everything I'd done as an actor, I still hadn't appeared on a Broadway (or thereabouts) stage. The week before 9/11, I got the part.

The first week of rehearsals, I wasn't having any fun. I just couldn't find my way into the role. And I remember we had a Saturday rehearsal on September 8, 2001. We finished rehearsing, and I was standing outside the theater next to the leading actress, a woman who had won an Oscar but couldn't remember her lines. She was waiting for her limo driver and just kind of babbling away. I don't even know what she was saying. Her limo pulled up, and she got in.

And I remember standing there, and, for some reason I cannot explain, I looked up at the sky and said, "I'm done. I'm done acting." And I went to Grand Central and took the train home.

Our next scheduled rehearsal was on Tuesday, September 11, 2001. I called the director and said, "You have three-and-a-half weeks of rehearsals left. I'd like to ask you to replace me." He tried to explain that the first week was always tough, things would get better, blah, blah.

But I repeated my request, knowing full well I was burning a bridge for life. And I hung up. And within minutes the first plane hit the World Trade Center, and this time we *all* fell into a rabbit hole, and the world would never be the same.

As for the show? It opened on a Saturday and closed on Sunday. On the front page of the Sunday *New York Times* arts section was a scathing three-quarter-page review. I felt whole and complete and done with performing. Can't explain it, but that's what happened.

WHAT I LEARNED ALONG THE WAY

My years of intensely pursuing an acting career opened my eyes to many truths that have become integral to my life.

HOW TO BEND TIME

When I said earlier that my pursuit of acting taught me how to bend time, I wasn't kidding.

I bent time by breaking the common belief that the harder you work, the more you produce and the more you earn. The key was pursuing what I loved.

People use the linear, quantitative concept of time as an excuse not to pursue their dreams. They look at their calendar and say, "I work forty-five hours a week. I spend ten hours a week commuting and five hours a week in the gym. On weekends and evenings, I have to spend time with my spouse and kids, take care of my elderly parents, work a volunteer job, do household projects, shop for groceries, cook, clean, pay my bills … Mathematically, there just isn't time to pursue a passion career. Someday, maybe. Not now.

I challenge you to flip that script. Put your passion pursuit first. Then see what happens to the rest of your time. You will discover—I promise you—that time bends in such a way that you're able to get all the same things done that you were doing before. At least the important ones. *And* you'll earn at least as much money as before, probably more.

Just the other day, I was talking to a writer who works fifty hours a week doing writing projects for others and has a busy nonwork schedule as well. He always wanted to write novels, but for years he used the excuse that there just wasn't enough time and energy in his week to write novels on top of his bread-and-butter writing. Then one day he simply stopped the excuses and started working on a novel. In three years' time, he has managed to write two novels—long ones at that—and get them published. Meanwhile, he suffered no loss in his regular income and now has the added income (and satisfaction) from the novels as well. Time bent for him, allowing him to do the "impossible."

I find that most people waste the precious time they have on this planet doing the immediate but not the essential, the important but not the significant, the necessary but not the consequential. And they remain stuck in linear time, complaining, "If only I had more time, I would get more done ..."

But the truth I discovered when working full time in both the theater and in finance was the reverse: when I do more, I *create* more time.

FIGHT *FOR* SOMETHING

Actors often struggle with how to make their performances credible and dynamic. "What's my motivation in this scene?" they'll ask directors.

A lesson I learned early on in acting is to always frame the question as "What am I fighting *for*?" When you find a positive motivation for your character, you unlock the secret of how to perform the scene.

That positive motivation can be anything from obvious goals such as I'm fighting to win the girl or I'm fighting to solve the crime to more subtle ones such as I'm fighting to bolster my self-image.

Even a walk-on role can be enlivened by adopting a "fighting for" attitude. The butler serving tea? Maybe he's fighting to preserve old-world traditions in which he still has value. The pizza delivery guy? Maybe he's fighting to be seen as someone important. Actors who adopt a "fight for" mentality bring Stanislavski's adage to life: "There are no small parts, only small actors."

The "fighting for" approach extends well beyond theater. I've discovered it to be an important principle in life as well. Instead of positioning yourself *against* the things you *don't* want—which is a negative motivation—ask yourself what goals and values you are trying to *champion*. And then fight for those and forget about what everyone else is doing.

Seriously. Try this. Our world today is locked in battles *against*. We are enormously divided as a species. We spend most of our energy demonizing others and trying to prove the other camp wrong. But that's a waste of time. Instead, ask, "What am I fighting for?" and act on that.

Let's say, for example, you believe people in the other "camp" are selfish and unkind. Rather than trying to build a case against their unkindness, make the decision to fight *for* kindness. Go out every day and treat people kindly. Perform acts of kindness. Don't waste another minute pointing fingers at those you perceive to be unkind.

Be a hero to someone else for a while, and see how it transforms your soul and your relationship to time. You won't need a cape, but you will take to the skies. I can attest to this from firsthand experience.

Literally anything you find yourself fighting *against* can be flipped into a fight *for*—and with world-changing results.

SIX

COACHING AND KIDS: GOD LOVES A VACUUM

Standing on that sidewalk, watching that actress get into her cab, was one of those moments in life when you feel whole and complete. There was no anger, no bitterness, no regret. I just knew I was finished with acting as a career—the auditions, the directors, the memorizing scripts written by others. I was done being a creative cog in someone else's machine.

I wasn't finished with stage performance, it turned out, not by a long shot. I was just done with pursuing the life of a professional actor for hire.

I have an expression: God loves a vacuum. If you don't fill it, she'll happily fill it for you. So I took a year to do nothing but work in my business. But that space I created in my life opened a new door. And within a year or so, I was back "on stage" again. In a whole new way ...

GOD AND TUNA SANDWICHES

I had a friend, Jeff McEwan, who was a senior VP at MassMutual, the company where I started my financial career. He and I had met a few years earlier at a conference, and we hit it off. We began this custom of meeting once a month, on a Tuesday, at a little Italian restaurant called Romitos, not far from my office in East Longmeadow. We would order tuna fish sandwiches and talk about what we really wanted to do next in our lives.

Jeff wanted to go out and start his own consulting company. Me, I was participating in an entrepreneurial coaching program called "Strategic Coach®," created by a brilliant futurist named Dan Sullivan. I was noodling with the idea of coaching financial advisors. But I wasn't sure how.

After about a year and a half of eating those tuna fish sandwiches, I finally said to Jeff, "You're cute and all, but we need to stop meeting like this. We should either get a room and create a real stir in this boring neighborhood or call it off." For Jeff creating a stir meant quitting his secure job and starting his own consulting company. And that's what he did.

I continued running my financial advising business, but I kept in touch with Jeff. Around 2002 the largest accounting firm in town approached me and said, "We're getting into the financial services business. In a big way. We're interviewing you and three other financial advising firms in town to select a partner to help us do that."

I was pumped. This was a huge opportunity for my firm to achieve a whole new level of success. At the time, we were getting most of our referrals by way of a weekly newsletter we sent out via *fax machine* (yup). I walked into the office of my business partner, a guy named Ray who was ten years my senior, and excitedly broke the news about the potential deal.

Ray looked at me without expression and said, "I don't like it."

"What do you mean, you don't like it?"

"If we partner with that accounting firm, every other accounting firm in town will stop referring us business."

I knew we weren't getting much business from those guys anyway. "I tell you what," I said to him. "Do some digging over the weekend. Go back five years and tell me how many referrals we've gotten from all those other accounting firms. And we'll talk again Monday morning."

Monday morning I walked into Ray's office and asked for his tally. Turned out, in five years we'd gotten five business referrals from accounting firms. Five, count 'em.

But Ray, for some reason I couldn't fathom, still didn't want to partner with the big accounting firm.

"Then *this* partnership is over," I said to him. "Go clean out your office, please."

Within two weeks I was working with the new firm.

THE 401(K) COACH

Once I began working with the new guys, I became intrigued with a part of their business they weren't paying much attention to: helping clients manage retirement plans. I sensed potential growth there. So I went to the managing partner and said, "Let's work together to build a benefit company to administer retirement plans. We can use it as a way to acquire 401(k) business, which I think is a gold mine."

He said, "Sure." And just like that, we both wrote a check to start Benefits Consulting Group LLC, a third-party retirement plan administrator (I know. Sexy, huh?). So I went back to Jeff, and he and I decided to launch a coaching program. Our idea was to teach financial advisors how to effectively drum up 401(k) business out there in the wilds of corporate America. We got twenty advisors to pay us $2,000 a year to do the first program.

Out of that first training, our benefit company acquired about a hundred new retirement plans. We were so profitable our first year in business that I gave the accountants all their risk capital back. And I was left alone to manage and grow the company.

I became "the 401(k) Coach," the face and voice of the operation, and over the next fifteen years, we trained over ten thousand advisors around the country in how to do what we were doing in our business. I was Duncan Hines selling my recipes to Betty Crocker. Our business took off like the space shuttle.

Using the Strategic Coach model I learned with Dan Sullivan, we designed a one-year program where we met with each group of advisors every ninety days for a year. I wrote the course for the first ninety days, and that's all we had to start with. Then I had ninety days to write the next ninety days, and so on. I was creating the program on the fly, hoping I had enough material to last me a year. Then, toward the end of the first year, our client companies started asking us, "What do you have next?" So, naturally, I told them, "Oh, we have a year-two program." We didn't, of course. I had to create that.

The 401(k) Coach program was an enormous success, right from the get-go, but sometimes, just like a no-name actor, you need that "big break" that puts your business into the stratosphere. Ours came in the form of a call from Texas. Everything's bigger in Texas, right?

BIG BREAK

For the first three years of 401(k) Coach, we were running most of our programs in Hartford, Connecticut, at the airport. Advisors would fly in every ninety days, take their course, and fly out again. Then one day we got a call from a 401(k) internal wholesaler in Texas—yes, there are wholesalers in the 401(k) industry—asking if we would come to Texas and put on our 401(k) Coach program there. We were finally getting noticed! We said, "If you put thirty advisors' 'cheeks' in the seats, we'll fly down there." And we promptly raised our tuition from $2,000 to $5,000. When you're in demand, we learned, raise your prices … a lot!

We started traveling to Texas every ninety days and putting on our program there for the enhanced fee. About three months after we started, I was on a panel (I was doing a lot of public appearances by then), and a guy by the name of Michael Butler was on it with me. He was the national head of all sales for Nationwide 401(k) plans. At this time, Nationwide *owned* the 401(k) industry; they were the giants. Butler said to me, "Hey, why don't you fly out to Columbus, and let's talk about how we might be able to work together?"

This was like the Wizard of Oz telling me, "Come to Emerald City, and I will make your dreams come true." I had been trying to get that invitation from Michael Butler for three years.

I couldn't get him to book that flight fast enough.

Walking into Butler's Columbus office with my assistant, "the Dog"—a nickname Hillary Ducharme, my first 401(k) Coach employee, had earned in college for her volleyball skills—*was* like walking into Oz. The room was the size of a football field, with a huge desk in one area, a golf green and a pool table in another area, couches, and a cappuccino machine in another. I'm pretty sure the place had its own post office and Dunkin' Donuts. Michael Butler beamed in on a ray of light—that's how I remember it anyway; I could be wrong—and invited us to sit on the couches to have a chat.

After we ordered our drinks from the hospitality robot and got a Shiatsu massage (I may be fuzzy about those details too), Michael turned to us and said, "So, who are you guys, and what do you do exactly?"

He had no clue who we were or why he had invited us. He had no idea that his number one, number two, and number three wholesalers were sponsoring us to travel to Texas four times a year to work with them or any notion about what we were teaching their advisors.

The response I gave to his question was a huge business lesson for me. Instead of launching into a one-sided spiel about myself and my company and how wonderful we were, I said, "Before I answer that question, can I ask *you* a question?"

"Sure," he replied.

I posed a question to Butler that I had learned from Dan Sullivan. He calls it the The R-Factor Question®. The R stands for relationship. "Michael," I said, "if it was three years from today and you and I were sitting here looking back on those three years, what would need to have happened for you to be satisfied with your progress, both personally and professionally?"

Silence ensued. Minutes literally passed. Finally, Butler looked at me and said, "Wow. No one has ever asked me a question like that before."

This was a guy who was accustomed to people asking *him* for things. And now here was this virtual stranger asking for nothing—just inviting him to talk about his bigger future. And talk he did. He told me he wanted to triple the size of his business. He talked about organizational changes he wanted to make. He talked about goals for his life and his family. He went on for twenty minutes as the Dog and I exchanged delicious smiles.

"Thank you for answering that question," I said when he was done. "May I ask one more?" He nodded. "Given that bigger future you describe—especially the part about tripling the size of your 401(k) business—what are the greatest dangers or obstacles you face, which, if eliminated, would most accelerate your success?"

"Man, that's another great question," he said. He sat there thinking, for what felt like five minutes, and then he launched into a detailed explanation of his greatest business challenges. In summary he said, "My biggest danger is that I'm not giving my mutual fund companies enough exposure to advisors." Then he stopped speaking, looked at me, and said, "Say, what is it you're doing down there in Texas?"

I told him.

He looked at me and said, "Hmm, would you do your program in seven more cities? *That's* how I can give my mutual fund companies more exposure to advisors!"

And that was it. I had solved his biggest danger. And all I'd done was listen.

We were off to the races. We started doing our one-year program in seven more cities. Michael Butler and Nationwide put us on the map. Oh, and the value of that one-year deal? $1 million.

Thank you, Marshall Wooper! Only I didn't need to borrow it, 'cause they were paying it to us!

That was my life for the next twelve years—flying around the country and being "the 401(k) Coach" for rooms full of eager advisors. I was the producer, writer, and entertainer. I was doing theater again—playing characters, telling stories, working a room, getting laughs—but for a purpose: helping people succeed. We were the only game in town, and companies were writing us million-dollar-a-year checks to travel around the country and coach their advisors. It was challenging, always having to iterate and adjust to the demands of the market by creating new content, products, and services, but I was loving it. My ego was loving it too. When some of the biggest financial companies in the world are hungry to hear what comes out of your mouth, it's heady stuff. For several years I made the "top 100 most influential individuals in the 401(k) industry" list. I was in demand.

We kept doing our program until about 2008, and then the stock market crashed, and nobody wanted to write a check for a million dollars. So we adapted. We created a one-day boot camp and did some other innovative stuff. And we continued to be successful for a while, but the industry was changing. Suddenly, everybody was a coach. When we'd started the company in 2002, nobody was doing what we were doing. But now, twelve years later, we were no longer operating in a blue ocean. It was all red ocean, and everyone was competing with us on price or giving their coaching away for free.

The last three years, we actually lost money. I should have shut it down sooner, but my ego couldn't let go of being the 401(k) Coach. Who would I be if not that guy?

It had been a hell of a run though. And I got a taste of what it feels like to put all your gifts together. Writer, producer, and performer—as well as wastebasket emptier, paper clip counter, "ticket seller," and everything in between. It was Monmouth Theater all over again … and I was loving it all. "Wonderment joy, laughter, play, and discovery for discovery's sake!"

AND NOW FOR SOMETHING COMPLETELY DIFFERENT: KIDS

During this same period of my life—starting with my early marriage and theater years—another major storyline was unfolding. It was another great illustration of "God loves a vacuum."

The vacuum in this case was the lack of children in my marriage. Both my wife Ellen and I wanted kids. But they weren't showing up. It didn't occur to me at the time that our "emptiness" on the child front was symptomatic of our marriage itself. Nor did I realize that God had *placed* this vacuum in our lives so she could fill it in the most extraordinary way.

At the time, we viewed our childlessness only as a problem to be solved, and we were busily trying to solve it. This meant fertility testing. For both of us.

GOOD SWIMMERS, BUT …

I remember the first time I got tested. I don't know if you've ever observed men in the waiting room of a fertility clinic, but you've never seen such ardent devotion to magazines. Everyone's trying to disappear behind a *Newsweek* or *Sports Illustrated*. So just to shake things up, after I went into the private room to do my business, I came bursting back into the office and plopped my vial down on the counter. "Look at that," I said to the receptionist. "Full to the brim. Do I get extra points for that?" I turned to look at the other guys waiting there, but they didn't seem to appreciate my humor. Go figure.

When I met with the urologist, I asked him, "So how'd I do, Doc?"

"I looked at your sample under the microscope," he said in his dignified Indian accent. "And you have a lot of swimmers …"

"That's good, right?"

"But they're not very strong swimmers!"

I was certain *I* wasn't the problem in this fertility scenario, so I said, "Prove it."

He led me down to the room with the microscope. I looked in the eyepiece and was surprised by what I saw. "I don't know about you, Doc, but there's a party going on down there. These guys are dancing and having a great time."

He looked into the 'scope and said, "Oh, my goodness. Looks like they've come alive under the warm light. I guess you're *not* the problem."

Neither was Ellen, though, as it turned out.

Still, no kid was showing up for us.

CHINA DESTINY

During this time my wife Ellen was a flight attendant, and she'd heard about this three-and-a-half-week cruise that went from Hong Kong to China to Korea to Japan. We decided to take it because she got a major discount. We ended up being the youngest couple on the trip. And for some mysterious reason, we became "children magnets." Everywhere we went in China, people would smile at us and hand us their children. So strange. We had booked the trip because we wanted to see China, but we fell in love with the *children* of China. We came home with about three hundred pictures of children—not the Great Wall, not the temples, not the pandas.

And since nobody was showing up for us, kid-wise, a no-brainer of an idea occurred. We should adopt a child from China.

And that's what we did. We went through a screening and application process, which took about a year, and then we flew over to China with five other couples for a two-week trip to meet and adopt our daughter. Talk about excitement. It was an amazing experience.

Of course there were the inevitable delays and setbacks before getting there. At one point China strafed Taiwan, and the US shut down diplomacy, and then China shut down adoption in turn. But that was all part of the process and the karma of it. Without the delays we probably wouldn't have ended up with our Hannah.

Hannah was born in southwestern China, a hundred miles north of the Vietnamese border, in a tiny town. They loaded six girls from her local orphanage, along with six women who worked there, onto a school bus and drove eight hours to a town called Kunming. It's known as the Spring City because of its beautiful weather.

The day we arrived in Kunming, we checked into the Holiday Inn, and the agency people greeted us. They said, "Unpack and clean up, and then we'll take you to a government building where you will meet your children. After that, *we* will take your children, and for the next ten days, we will do some sightseeing as a group …"

"Excuse me," I said. "What was that part about 'we'll meet our children and then you'll take them back'?"

"Yes, we'll take care of the children for the duration of your visit. And then we'll give them to you at the end of the ten days."

All the parents were looking at one another in confusion. I spoke up again (through a translator). "No, no. We see children, we *keep* children."

They seemed confused. Turns out our hosts had assumed we were all wealthy American couples (we weren't) who wouldn't want to be bothered changing diapers and feeding babies. So they'd brought the women from the orphanage along to care for the kids during our stay. Yeah, no. That wasn't going to work for us, and we told them so.

LOVE AT FIRST SIGHT

We went to the government building to meet our kids for the first time, and we were sitting in a room, waiting and waiting. Finally, some women walked by the doorway holding babies. As the last child passed, I saw her face. And I knew she was ours. I turned to Ellen and said, "That's Hannah." We knew our daughter out of the six kids.

Without announcement the women swept into the room. Six women holding six kids. And we all just froze. No one knew what to do.

There was a table in front of the room, and I remember one of the women took a baby and stood her up on the table. And she was looking around like ET stepping out of his spaceship. And she was our daughter. Finally, my paralysis broke, and I crawled over to her and just lightly touched her toes. And then, one by one, the other parents unfroze and came over. And they each took a child and held it. And then joy broke out, all at once. What a moment that was. Six sets of parents, all meeting their children for the very first time. Together.

THE LUCKY ONES

The first night we were in the hotel, a remarkable thing happened. We came downstairs, and our hosts told us they had a room set up for our dinner. But there was a wedding going on in the ballroom, and we would need to walk through it to get to our room.

As we started to walk through this big ballroom, the whole wedding party stopped and parted like the Red Sea. And everyone broke into spontaneous applause—because these were the lucky children. They were going to America. And that was cause for celebration in China. At least in those days; maybe that has changed.

We walked through that room like royalty, and we felt like it. We knew *we* were the lucky ones.

MORE GOOD FORTUNE

Our luck continued from there. The next morning we all met for breakfast. And of course, everybody wanted to share their "first night" horror stories. "Nina was up three times." "Sydney was up five times, coughing and throwing up."

"What about Hannah?"

"Um, she slept through the night," was our reply.

Our daughter slept through every night of our stay in China. By the third morning, none of the other parents wanted to sit with us anymore.

Every day we'd all get on a yellow school bus and visit a different place. One day we went to the circus, another day we visited the Stone Forest, a famous geological feature about sixty miles southeast of Kunming. Everywhere we went the Chinese people were so welcoming and so happy to see the children.

FINAL HITCHES

Things went smoothly for us all, the whole trip. Except for one major glitch. We'd been told American Express checks would be fine when it came to making our final payment to the orphanage. So that's what everybody was carrying. Not I, though. My feeling was, "Cash is always king." I had a money belt with $30,000 US in it. I didn't bring any American Express checks.

The third day of the trip, news broke that somebody was forging American Express checks in China. So the orphanage was no longer going to accept them. That meant every day we had to make a stop at the Bank of China so the other parents could cash some of their AmEx checks. The problem was the government would only cash $500 a day. We weren't going to be in China long enough for them to accumulate the $15,000 needed for the final payment.

The last night arrived, and we had to make the final payment to the orphanage. Somehow, I got appointed chief negotiator. All the parents were in one room and the Chinese orphanage people were in another, and I just kept going back and forth, haggling over how much they would take in American Express checks.

It turned into a marathon negotiation, but we finally got everyone settled up. More or less. But I remember flying out late that night to

Guangzhou, where the American consulate was, wondering if soldiers were going to storm the plane when we landed and take the kids back.

Guangzhou is on the eastern coast, and it's miserable. We went from 75 degrees to 105 in the shade, but that wasn't our main problem. You see, while we were in China, President Bill Clinton had signed the Anti-Terrorism Bill. So when we arrived at the American consulate the next morning to get passports and paperwork for the kids to take them home, a woman behind a sheet of bulletproof plexiglass told us, "Not so fast." The antiterrorism act stated that no foreign national could come to the United States until their passport had cleared for two weeks.

"Your *children* are foreign nationals," the woman behind the plexiglass informed us. "Therefore, they can't leave for at least two weeks."

I couldn't believe what I was hearing. "Hang on," I said to her, not very cordially. I stormed away from her window and ran downstairs and out the door. One of the other husbands, Rich, was with me, and he was looking at me as if I had lost my mind. The other parents were waiting outside in the heat with the babies. I looked at Ellen and said, "Give me Hannah."

She reluctantly handed the baby to me, and I ran back up the stairs to Plexiglass Patty. I stood Hannah on the counter and said, "*This* is my eight-month-old terrorist. You wanna check her for bombs and weapons?"

Plexiglass Patty got flustered and said, "Wait here."

She bustled off to a back room and was gone for about twenty minutes. The whole time Rich was looking at me like *I* was the terrorist, but I was holding my ground for all of us and our new daughters! Finally, Patty returned and said, "Okay, we can get half of you out tomorrow, but the other half will need to stay another three days. Best I can do."

Rich and I went back downstairs and told the others, "We have to draw straws. There's six families. Three can go, three have to stay." It was the only fair thing to do, but I felt bad for Rich. He and his wife had another kid at home, and they were burned out and homesick.

We picked straws, and Rich drew one of the short ones. The blood drained from his face.

I didn't say anything to Ellen. I just turned to Rich and handed him my long straw. I said, "Go home. Your daughter's waiting for her new sister. We have our whole family right here."

We stayed and enjoyed China for another three days, blissful in our new familyhood, happy to have played a role in the lives of Rich's family.

MORE KID MAGIC

Hannah came home, and she was so easy. Happy, energetic, smart, developing ahead of schedule. A couple of years later, we started talking about having another kid.

The story of our second child is even more synchronistic than Hannah's.

Ellen and Hannah wanted a daughter and a sister, respectively. But I said, "If nobody's showing up naturally, I get to choose. And I'm having a boy."

For the next couple of years, we went back and forth about it. And then one day I was shaving in the bathroom. And Hannah walked in—she was almost five—and said, "Dad, I'm ready for my brother now."

I laughed and, without thinking, I said, "Oh, what's his name?"

She said, "Noah," then turned on her heels and walked out.

After I finished shaving, I went downstairs and said to Ellen, "Have you heard about Noah?"

She replied, "Oh, last week we were getting in the car to go to the store. Hannah turned and said, 'Come on, Noah. Let's get in.' There was no one there."

We knew our son's name before we met him. Noah.

This time we decided to adopt from Vietnam, and we worked with the same agency.

Here's where it gets weirder. Before we had started the adoption process, I had heard from a friend of mine who had cycled through Vietnam with Butterfield & Robinson, the adventure-travel company. So in summer of 2001, I booked a solo trip to cycle for two weeks through Vietnam. My departure was already ticketed for January 15, 2002.

In September of 2001, we started the adoption process. On November 12, Noah was born, and two weeks later we received the photos. Things were about to get real. Now, when you're adopting from Vietnam, unlike China, you have to go there twice. The first time, they meet you, you go to the orphanage, you see your baby, you count their toes, and you fill out some paperwork. And then you have to leave the country. Why, I don't know. Two months later, you come back to take the child home. That's how they do it.

Ellen said, "*I'm* not going over there. Because there's no way I could see him and leave."

Guess that meant *I* was going. I felt like Tonto in the *Lone Ranger* shows—"Hey, Tonto, you go to town and get beat up by the bad guys, then come back and report what you found!" In December I got a phone call, and they said, "We've got a group going to Vietnam in January to see the kids."

I said, "When are they traveling?"

"Well, you would fly out on January 15 and arrive on January 16."

I already had my tickets, purchased six months earlier: departing on January 15, arriving in Vietnam on the sixteenth.

It was as if my son had somehow orchestrated all this. "Hey, Dad, I know you're gonna be in Vietnam anyway. Maybe you can stop in and see me in the orphanage. We'll get to know each other a bit, and then you can hop on your bike and go see my country." And that has been my son's disposition his whole life—laid back and easy.

So I flew over in January with my already-bought ticket. I went to the orphanage for three hours with the other ten couples, and I met my son. Later, they drove me up to Da Lat to catch up with my cycling group. And I spent the next ten days cycling from Da Lat to Hanoi, soaking in the sights, sounds, foods, and people of my son's native country. Incredible.

I came home and then, six weeks later, Ellen, Hannah, and I went back to Vietnam and stayed for two weeks in an apartment complex with the other adopting families. We had another amazing time, and then we brought Noah home.

Unlike my daughter, my son *never* slept through the night. For nine months he'd wake up with night terrors, and I would go into his room and just touch him, and he would go back to sleep. When my finger came off him, he'd sit up screaming. What could have happened to a kid so young to bring out that kind of terror? We'd never know. All we could do was love him.

Adopting my kids was the blessing of a lifetime and a miraculous experience, but it was also the beginning of an ending. By the time Noah set foot on American soil, I knew my marriage was over. It was just a question of how and when to end it.

WHAT I LEARNED ALONG THE WAY

This period of my life was one of immense growth. Some of the things I learned in both business and life:

LISTENING IS MORE POWERFUL THAN SPEAKING

Every good actor learns that "acting is listening." *Business* is listening too. Unfortunately, most businesspeople never learn this lesson.

Practically all the training we receive in business school, and even in communication school, revolves around the act of *presenting*—talking, selling, marketing, getting *your* agenda on the table so you can sell more products and do more business.

But when I got that huge training contract from Michael Butler, I didn't get it by talking. I got it by asking two thoughtful, probing questions, and then *really listening* to what he had to say. He eventually talked himself to the place where he realized he needed my services without my needing to do one minute of salesman song and dance.

No one enjoys being "sold" anything. A listening-and-discovery process is infinitely more engaging. Think about yourself. When choosing a store to shop in, do you prefer the one where a salesman attacks you the minute you walk in the door or the one where the staff strike up a natural conversation and ask *you* about what *your* needs are?

Everyone likes being listened to. When another person listens to us, we feel honored and respected. We feel as if we matter to that person. We feel a connection with a fellow human being. We feel appreciation toward that person for giving us the time and platform to talk about our problems and desires. All these things form the basis of liking and trusting. And liking and trusting are the main reasons we choose to do business with someone.

On the other hand, when someone preaches or lectures or "presents to" us, we feel a bit used. We know we don't matter to that person. All that matters to them is *their* agenda, not ours. And why would we want to do business with someone like that?

Why would we want to be in any kind of relationship with someone like that?

True listening doesn't happen with just the ears. It involves opening up a space for another soul in our hearts and in our being. And this opening up is the key to success in all relationships—marriage, parenthood, friendship, business, even pet owner to pet.

NOTHING EVER GOES WRONG

Most of us spend our lives trying to make sure things go right for us and prevent things from going wrong. When we're not actively pushing buttons toward those ends, we're preoccupied with *hoping* things go right and *worrying* they'll go wrong.

But one thing my life has taught me—the adoptions in particular—is that we can never say, with assurance, that anything has ever gone wrong. We haven't seen the whole picture yet, so how can we know? The greatest things that happen in our lives are often a direct or indirect result of something having gone horribly "wrong" beforehand.

My children wouldn't have come to my life without such "negatives" as my bad marriage to the wrong person (see next chapter), unwanted pregnancies, bureaucratic snafus and delays, years of infertility struggles, and a million other factors *I would have changed if I'd had control.*

Thank God we humans are not at the helm. If we were, we would mess everything up. In our desire to avoid short-term inconvenience and pain, we would "fix" every problem before it happened, thus shutting the door on all the long-term blessings that are trying to work their way into our lives.

The best approach, I've found, is to stay open to "the flow of life," embrace unforeseen outcomes, and accept whatever actually happens, trusting that it's "all good" in the end.

Dividing the world into positive and negative aspects puts our happiness at the whim of circumstance. On days when things appear to be going our way, we're happy. On days when things seem to be going "wrong," we're stressed and miserable. But it's all a myopic illusion. We never know when a seemingly terrible event might actually be the best thing that ever happened to us.

Instead of basing our happiness, conditionally, on external events, why not make an *internal* decision to be open and available to life and to be more accepting of the unknown—that which we can't see and don't even know to be true—regardless of what unfolds in our outer world? Why not surrender management of our futures to an intelligence higher than our own—one that does a much better job than we could ever hope to?

SEVEN

MARRIAGE: WAR AND PEACE

As I said in the last chapter, nothing "goes wrong." As long as you don't let the bad stuff knock you out of the game, it always leads you to a better place, eventually. Of course, at the actual moment you're drowning in excrement, it doesn't always feel that way.

Speaking of drowning in excrement, let's talk about my divorce and first marriage! I need to be careful here. I don't want to fall into the temptation of demonizing my ex-wife or violating her privacy. So I will speak only in general terms, and I will acknowledge, up front, that I was at least equally responsible for the failure of the marriage. I was a crap husband.

Many things can doom a marriage—money problems, infidelity, dishonesty—but one of the biggest wedges that can cleave couples in two is when the two people are on different life trajectories. If one party is oriented toward growth and expansion and the other is content to remain in an eternal comfort zone, eventually a rip is going to occur. Take it from me.

AN INNOCENT START

My marriage started the way most do, with a spark. I first noticed Ellen when I was still in college working for Hillard Aronson and he and I went to a restaurant called Ichabod's. Ellen was waiting tables— long, blond hair, attractive. And remember, this was Springfield, not Manhattan, so the number of attractive people in your age range was finite. They stuck in your mind.

A year or two later, I went into this other eatery called the Keg Room, next door to my office, for lunch. And there she was again, tending bar. This time I didn't choose to remain silent. I walked right up to her and said, "Wanna have lunch sometime?" Smooth, I know.

Her reply was, "In case you hadn't noticed, I work during lunch." Oh, right. But then she surprised me with, "Why don't you take me to dinner instead?"

The rest is painful history.

MISMATCHED

It should have been obvious from the start we weren't a good match, but I was young and thinking with parts of my anatomy not designed for thought.

Ellen's life consisted of tending bar and partying with her friends. Me, I was all about the future and trying to build a business. Our lives didn't align. On the plus side, she was fun and effervescent, like my mother had been, and she knew a lot of people in town I didn't know. We moved in together within six months—into that apartment on Hamburg Street, where we struggled to pay the rent and the heat.

Eventually, she went to work for the airlines as a flight attendant, and I started doing well in my business. Things improved for us financially, but not emotionally.

THE EST YEARS

What should have broken us up before we even went the marriage route was my decision to take the est training. If you're old enough to remember est—before it morphed into the Forum and later the Landmark Forum—you may recall it was quite a challenging and eye-opening experience. The training took place over two consecutive weekends, and it was designed to do nothing less than transform your life. Est was famous for two things: not letting you pee except during designated bathroom breaks and calling you an asshole a lot. But it *worked*. It had the power to change ingrained behaviors and mindsets. For many people, me included, it eventually led to years of further self-examination and spiritual exploration.

Est was the best show in town, hands down. You never knew what was going to happen at an est event. I was blown away by the mastery of the trainers; they could handle anything that came up—and a lot of things came up. There was one famous incident, for example, where Werner Erhard himself was repeatedly tossed like a rag doll by a huge man who was feeling threatened, until the man broke down in tears like a child.

I remember at my first est event, the week two trainer, Charlene, just sat there staring at the three hundred participants for literally ten minutes before speaking a word. Fully present, fearless, completely unruffled. Who does that? Trainings would often go until three or four in the morning, then resume a few hours later.

It was guerrilla theater of the spiritual kind. I wanted in. Not just as a participant, but as a staffer.

The first step I took was to become a guest seminar leader. Guest seminars were short informational events designed to introduce people to est and get them to sign up for the full training. I was so bad at it, I led sixteen guest seminars in a row where nobody registered!

I knew I needed to go deeper, to find out what the trainers knew. So I started working my way up the food chain, from guest seminar leader to training supervisor. Training supervisors helped run the trainings and supported the trainers. From 1983–1985, I traveled around the country, working as an unpaid training supervisor. It was truly the best "entertainment" I had ever experienced—people are "bat-shit crazy" on the surface, but at their core they are whole, magnificent, and full of love. The training was all about getting them to give up the surface facade and bring their complete nature into the light.

A big part of est was getting people to keep their agreements with themselves and others. Because of this, a lot of participants got booted out of the training. They would do something to break a simple agreement, such as showing up late—the type of thing tolerated in most settings—and would be ejected. As a training supervisor, I had the job to make sure everybody who came to the training completed it. Even those who were thrown out. So I would have to go hunt these people down, make sure they understood the reason for their ejection, and get them to recommit. It made for some "spirited" exchanges.

I remember the day I really found my power in est. They flew me out to California for the second weekend of a training in LA. The trainer was a psychotherapist named Nancy. The first night of the training, we were at the Ambassador Hotel. Around midday, we were told by the staff that we would have to pack everything up at the end of the day and bring it to the Holiday Inn in Hollywood for day two. Well, day one didn't finish till about one thirty in the morning. And then we had to pack up and move a half hour away. Huge hassle—everyone was exhausted.

In the middle of packing up, things weren't going well, and the room supervisor lost it. He screamed, "I've had enough!" and ran off into the woods. We finally found him and dragged him back, and then managed to get to the Holiday Inn at two thirty. By the time we set everything up, it was four o'clock. I sent everybody home to get three hours of sleep and be back by eight o'clock. The training was set to start at ten.

Next morning all the est staffers did come back, to my surprise. But I wasn't happy with how things had gone, so I called half of them to the front of the room and had them sit in the front row. "You're all fired," I said. "Go home."

Nancy, the trainer, was in the back of the room, along with the rest of the est staff. They all stopped talking at once, and their mouths fell open. Nancy smiled; she knew what I was doing.

One of the est staffers asked why they were fired, and I said, "Because none of you got your job done yesterday. Does any of you know what your job is?"

People gave answers like "run the microphones" and "clean the toilets."

"No," I said, "those are not your jobs. Your job is to make the room supervisor look great. And last night he ran off into the woods. He did not look great. You didn't get your job done. So you're all fired. Nancy and I will run the microphones today, and we'll give people what they came for—a transformed life."

Everyone was in shock. I let them steep in that feeling for a bit, and then I finally said, "I'll tell you what I'm gonna do. I'll give you five minutes to think about this." Nobody moved. I walked to the back of the room. I looked at the rest of the est staffers—I was only a volunteer myself—and said, "I *own* every one of you for this whole day. You're mine. I don't care what job you do, I own your ass. Is that clear?" Nancy had a big grin on her face but didn't say a word. And then I walked back to the front of the room and said, "You're all still here. There must be a reason for that. One by one, I will give you a chance to recommit to what you're here for." Everyone recommitted and stayed.

It was one of those all-in, come-to-Jesus moments where there's no backing down. I was either going to win or I was going to lose big. My confidence somehow bent the room to my will.

And Nancy led one of the most amazing trainings, which I supervised, and not one person got thrown out or left!

That's the kind of stuff that happened all the time at est. You had to be fully present to your power, command, and ownership from moment to moment to moment—kind of like Sandy Meisner's belief about acting: an actor lives truthfully in imaginary circumstances by living, breathing, and speaking from moment to moment to moment.

FAULT LINES IN THE RELATIONSHIP

Everyone in my family did the est training—my brother, my sister, even my dad. Ellen did it, too, but it was a one-time thing for her. She didn't take it any further. And that should have been the "tell," right there, that we were walking different roads.

I don't mean to suggest that the road I walked was pure and heroic, by the way. It wasn't. I fell into the trap of many est insiders. I became arrogant and took advantage of my status. In those days women would throw themselves at you when you were an est leader— the confidence, the swagger. I fell in love with a woman in Boston eleven years my senior and began living two lives for a while. What I should have done was just be honest with Ellen and split up. But instead I soldiered on in my relationship with her, out of guilt and misplaced responsibility.

Ellen and I got married in 1985, and by 1990 it was abundantly clear that this was a bad idea. We argued constantly. I didn't respect her; she didn't respect me. At bottom we just wanted different things out of life and each other.

By the time the kids arrived, our marriage was on life support. For a while the joy of playing parents distracted us. But when Noah was three and Hannah was eight, both Ellen and I agreed we couldn't go on, and I decided to move out. Noah wanted to come with me. Hannah was devastated, and I don't think she ever fully recovered.

D-I-V-O-R-C-E

It took a hell of a lot more time and money to get *out* of the marriage than it had taken to get into it, let me tell you. When people ask me to describe my divorce, I say, "Easy: five lawyers, five judges, five guardians ad litem, and five point five million dollars." I walked out in '03, we got officially divorced in '07, and we were in that courtroom every damn year until 2019. Our divorce lasted almost as long as our marriage.

I still can't believe how adversarial and ridiculous things became. I remember, after three years of watching the lawyers on both sides playing games and posturing and racking up their bills, we finally made it into a courtroom. Thank God. Then I watched for an hour and a half as my lawyer and her lawyer squabbled in front of this judge. It was like watching my wife and me, always trying to one-up each other or defend our mutually destructive points of view. The judge finally said, "Enough! You've been working on this for three years, and you haven't been able to get it resolved. You're in my courtroom now, and *I'm* gonna get it done."

Whew. I was delighted to know a resolution would be coming. We were given a trial date one month out. And then, a week later, I found out my wife hired a new shark attorney to team up with her previous attorney. And they went to the judge and told him they couldn't be ready for trial in a month. Seriously? After three years of dickering and depositions?

The judge caved. He allowed my wife to hire the new shark lawyer and to start all over again, with new depositions, the whole works. Within six weeks, the shark had spent more money than our original two lawyers had in three years.

This clown was firing out subpoenas like a T-shirt cannon. He actually subpoenaed the CEO, CFO, and head of HR for Mass-Mutual, a Fortune 100 company, for depositions—because I had done business with the company. Ridiculous.

Finally, we went to court. On the first day, my lawyers—we each now had two lawyers, by the way—said to me, "You're probably going on the witness stand today. So be ready."

I was on the witness stand for *six hours*. They tried to prove I was hiding resources from my wife, which I wasn't. They came at me from all sides, but they weren't able to crack me, because there was nothing *to* crack. And the judge was obviously getting tired of it.

The next morning my lawyers told me, "They want to talk with you." Negotiate a deal. Because they knew they were losing. And so we went to work, both sides, trying to hammer out an agreement—something we should have done three years and a million dollars earlier.

Negotiations went on from nine in the morning to two in the afternoon. Finally, my attorneys said, "Let's go back into the courtroom and let the judge decide how to divide up your assets.

I looked at my two lawyers and said, "All right, you want to go back in the courtroom, fine. But just remember one thing: this woman, Ellen, actually believes that if she were to pour kerosene on her body right now and light herself on fire, it would do more harm to me than it would to her!" That got my lawyers' attention, and they decided to continue negotiations. The courtroom was supposed to close at five o'clock, but the judge kept it open late, and at quarter of six, we stood in front of him, and we *finally* signed off on an agreement.

And for the next seven years, we were in and out of court, fighting over every frigging detail.

MEETING SWAMI

Here is where we catch up with the story I started at the beginning of the book.

As we were going through the divorce, I was building my 401(k) Coach business, as you may recall. My schedule would go something like this: I'd have the kids Monday and Tuesday. Wednesday, I would fly out to some city, somewhere in the US, with Marie Forest, my assistant, and another employee. I would spend all day Thursday in a room with fifty to a hundred financial advisors, coaching them on how to grow their 401(k) business. Then I'd fly back Friday morning and see the kids on the weekend. So I was on the road pretty much the entire three-and-a-half years we were trying to get the divorce finalized.

Instead of slowing down my financial growth, like most people do when going through a divorce, I was ramping up—growing both my advising business and my 401(k) coaching business. My work was rejuvenating to me. Being with my kids was rejuvenating too. But the rest of the time, I was in hell, feeling like my organs were being ripped out. As I described earlier, I would wake up in a strange hotel room. I would do my yoga. I would meditate. And then I would burst out crying over what I was about to lose, financially and emotionally.

In the midst of my sobbing, my cell phone would ring, and it would be Marie Forest. She'd say, "You good?"

I would always respond, "Good."

And Marie would say, in a singing, sparkling voice, "I have your cappuccino. I'll see you downstairs."

I'd jump in the shower, wash away the tears, put on my suit, meet Marie in the lobby, and say, "It's show time!"

It was in the middle of this ripped-apart existence that Marie *Case* (the other Marie), who knew how much I was suffering, called me and said, "You need to get on a plane to Austin, Texas, and come to my house, pronto. Swami is coming."

A BIT ABOUT MARIE

Let me tell you a bit about Marie Case and our friendship, so you'll know why I jumped on that plane, despite my reservations. I met Marie back in 1980 when I was just starting out in business. I stopped into the print shop she ran in Northampton—a college town in western Massachusetts—to drop off a free atlas she had signed up to receive from me.

I walked in, and she was behind the counter running the offset machine. There was a line of student customers waiting to get their printing done. I introduced myself and told her I had her atlas. She laughed; clearly this was not a good time to deal with the likes of me. So I just jumped over the counter and started waiting on her customers, as if I worked there. (Marie insists I was hitting on the coeds, but, to date, there is no physical evidence to support that assertion.)

We became fast friends as a result, and she bought life insurance from me. She also started referring me to her whole network of young entrepreneurs. So I felt a debt of gratitude to her.

A few years later, everybody was opening print shops, and Marie was getting squeezed out. She was in financial difficulty. I invited her to come to an est guest seminar in Boston. She came, and I could see she really wanted to do the training. But it cost a lot of money, and her finances were in the crapper, so I said, "I'll give you the money."

She refused my offer. But I wouldn't take no for an answer. Long story short: Marie took the training and became the poster child for a transformed life. Within a month she shut down her print shop. Within six months she moved to Boston. Lost over a hundred pounds. Within a year she was working for Werner Erhard's transformational technology company. She went on to become an enormously successful management consultant—living in London, consulting with Bechtel Corporation, calling me from CEOs' yachts, the works. She also became a training supervisor for est, like me, and we have traveled many lifetimes together.

Marie felt she owed me one because of what the training did for her life. And so ...

THE ENCOUNTER WITH SWAMI

Up the stairs of her castle turret I walked, with that folded-up piece of paper in my pocket. That piece of paper on which I had written, from the depths of my pain, my deepest and only desire.

Step.

Step.

Step.

I ascended into the upper room, and there he was. "Swami." Squatting on one of the two chairs. Not sitting but *squatting*. On his feet. Dressed in white, with a yellow silk scarf wrapped around him. Not an imposing figure, not a white-bearded guru type. Just a fairly slight, thirty-something guy with poofy hair whom you might see waiting tables at an Indian restaurant. On a dresser beside him were framed pictures of Jesus Christ, Mary, and an old guy I later learned was his guru, Baba.

He gestured for me to sit in the chair opposite him. I did, and we sat there for a minute or two, just kind of staring at each other. At last he said, "How can I be of service to you today?"

"I haven't a f**king clue," I replied. "I don't know who the f**k you are, and I don't know what the f**k I'm doing here."

Yep, those were my first words to a man I later learned was one of the world's greatest living spiritual masters.

Swami smiled. And then the anguish started pouring out of me. I told him all about the suffering I was going through and the guilt I was racked with for being such a shit in my marriage. On and on I went, unloading myself on this perfect stranger for about half an hour. By the end I was crying uncontrollably.

When I finally stopped, Swami stared at me and said, "Do you believe in Jesus Christ?"

Not what I'd been expecting to hear from an Indian master. I looked at the framed picture, then back at Swami, and said, "No disrespect, but he's not my guy. I mean I'm Jewish, right?"

Swami tossed his head back and laughed hysterically. I laughed hysterically too. Suddenly, we weren't master and disciple; we were just two guys sharing a massive belly laugh. I laughed harder than I had laughed in literally *years*, and I think that laugh did more to cleanse my soul than five years of prayer could have done.

At last he asked me, "So, what do you want?"

I took the piece of paper from my pocket, unfolded it, and looked at the single word I had written there. "Peace," I said to Swami. "All I want is peace. Can you give me that?"

Swami smiled again. He stood up in front of me and asked me to close my eyes. I did so, and seconds later I smelled incense. He gently asked me to put all my attention on my "third eye." And then I felt his arms moving around me, and he touched me on the forehead, in the spot believed to provide spiritual vision.

Suddenly, there was a burst of light, and I felt as if I were being propelled into the heavens. White light, white clouds, and a dizzying sensation—like I was flying on the wings of angels. My body was filled with light on the inside and wrapped in a blanket of warmth on the outside. A rush of emotion flowed through me. I felt completely safe and completely free, all at the same time. All my fears, all my anxieties, all my sadness, all my longing and despair were washed away in an instant. And I just started sobbing. And sobbing and sobbing. With no self-control or inhibition. I had never sobbed with such abandon. Or joy.

Finally, the tears stopped, and I heard Swami say, "You can open your eyes now."

I did, and he was standing in front of me, glowing with inner light. Then his body heaved, and he started choking as if he was gagging on something stuck deep in his belly. I knew, somehow, that he didn't need any help or medical intervention.

This gagging and choking went on for several minutes, and then he hunched over slightly, his mouth wide open, and cupped his hands in front of his chin. Out of his mouth popped a perfectly shaped, yellow "shiva lingam" stone, which he had produced from his body.

He handed it to me. It was clear, dry, and glistening. A solid rock. Then he moved behind me and said an old Indian prayer. Finally, he handed me the ashes of the rose petals he had been burning to create the incense smell.

"Carry these petals and this yellow lingam with you wherever you travel," he said, "and you will be surrounded with peace."

I had no clue what had just gone down. At the same time, I couldn't resist asking, "Aren't you going to give me a mantra to recite?" Someone had told me I'd be given one.

Smiling, Swami looked at me, waved his finger in a scolding way, and said "Oh no, no mantra for you."

We both laughed again, man to man. His words later became a private joke between us.

I thanked him and, stunned by what had just taken place, walked out of the room, down the stairs, and into the sunlight.

THE AFTERMATH

Marie rushed up to me and said in a shocked voice, "What have you been doing?"

"I've been sitting with Swami. Like you told me to do."

"Do you know how long you've been up there?"

"Not a fricking clue."

"Almost fifty minutes." Her tone was vaguely accusatory.

"Okay, if you say so."

"I don't think you understand what's going on here."

"Now that's the first bleeping thing you've said all day that makes any goddamn sense."

She went on to explain to me that devotees wait in line for hours, sometimes days, to get five minutes with Swami, and here I was, a "nonbeliever," getting nearly an hour. I couldn't explain it any more than I could explain what had happened in that room. Except that Swami and I had become fast friends.

While I was still at Marie's home, I was introduced to a very special woman named Monica Taylor. Monica was sitting in Marie's dining area when I came downstairs. I realized I had not eaten any food since my arrival late last night. Food was laid out beautifully in Marie's kitchen. I loaded up a plate and sat at the large, half-circular table near Monica. Monica greeted me with a warm smile. After a few minutes of gentle silence, she took out a small journal, opened it to a blank page, and said, "Please, will you draw me a picture of your home?"

Odd request, I thought, and yet everything that just happened to me upstairs was even odder. Had I perhaps stepped into the rabbit hole, like Alice in Wonderland? Monica handed me her journal and a pencil, and I began to outline the amazing property and home I had lived in for the past thirteen years. It was a thirteen-acre property, with a two-acre pond in the back, a two-acre pasture, and a five-stall horse stable. The home itself was a uniquely designed two-story house. Monica smiled as I drew and explained the property to her.

She asked, "Where does the sun rise?"

I enthusiastically showed her on the drawing. "It rises across the street in the morning, and then sets over the pond at the back of the property in a magnificent sunset!"

Unimpressed, she quietly said, "Bad vastu."

Before I could even digest the word or ask what it meant, she continued, "Have you ever lost any money living in this house?"

Again enthusiastically, I responded, "Lost money? To the contrary; for the past thirteen years, my income has done nothing but go up …" And then I paused as the meaning of her question hit me like a two-by-four. I went on, "But given the divorce firestorm I'm in, it's about to drop precipitously."

"Bad vastu," she repeated.

It was then I noticed Swami standing beside me at the dining room table. How long he had been there listening I did not know. He asked if he could sit with us for lunch and slid in between Monica and me. He then asked if I would like to see his ashram in India. I had the good fortune of sitting with him as he shared photos of his ashram on Marie's sixty-inch TV. It was magnificent. But one picture took my breath away. It showed *thousands* of people surrounding Swami as he led them through his teachings. Swami, who was also a prankster and loved to tell jokes, asked me how many people I thought were there.

I said, "Five, six thousand?"

He smiled and replied, "Fifty to one hundred thousand. They come every weekend." My jaw dropped as I realized the stature of the man I was in the presence of—and the enormity of the role these people bestowed on him. And every one of those people came with some type of suffering or pain they hoped Swami could help them wash away.

Swami then whispered something in my ear. Something I think he had been longing to share with another man, privately, for perhaps an eternity, to relieve *him* of some of his pain and suffering, or at least to be comprehended. It was, and still is, a sacred gift he shared with me. I shall forever be changed by it and remain the keeper of those sacred words.

I flew home that night. By the time my car pulled up to my house, it must have been about twelve thirty in the morning. As I was getting out of the car, I heard the phone ringing inside. I knew who it was.

Welcome back to reality. With a vengeance, I thought.

I sighed and walked through the front door. I didn't even turn the lights on. I picked up the ringing phone, and this time instead of screaming at me, she said quietly and gently, "Charlie, I'm done. I'm done. I'm done." And hung up the phone.

And I finally had it. Peace. "You and me, Swami," I said, looking up. "You and me."

WHAT I LEARNED ALONG THE WAY

Lessons learned at this time:

GET OFF YOUR STORY, OWN YOUR CHOICES

A huge lesson I learned through est (and also through meditation and other spiritual practices) was how to own the choices I make in my life. Most of us, when asked why we did something, immediately start running our storytelling machinery. We blame our past—or other people—for the choices we make. Instead of being accountable, we tell stories.

I remember in the est training an exercise called chocolate/vanilla. The trainer would pick out someone from the audience who was struggling with the material. They would bring this person to the front of the room and say, "I want you to imagine I'm holding an ice cream cone in each hand. One's vanilla and one's chocolate. Tell me which you choose." And the person would choose, say, chocolate. The trainer would hand her the imaginary chocolate ice cream cone and say, "Why do you choose chocolate?"

And the person would lapse into a story. "When I was seven years old, my dad brought me to this ice cream store ..."

Then the trainer would patiently say again, "Why do you choose chocolate?"

And the participant would dig deeper into the story file. "When I was two, I saw my mother eating a chocolate cone ..."

On and on this would go until the person ran out of stories and just said, "I choose chocolate because I choose chocolate." No reason. No story. Just a pure, free choice.

There's an immense freedom in making choices without the baggage of stories. "I want *x* because I want *x*. Because *x* is what calls me. I don't need to justify that choice to anyone or to myself." And once the choice is made, "I made that choice. Period." No rationalizations.

People sometimes ask me, "Why did you buy a Bentley?" and I always respond the same, "Because I always wanted a Bentley."

But that's not good enough for people. They come back and say, "Yeah, but *why* did you want a Bentley? Why, why, why?" As if any reason I gave them would satisfy them anyway.

To choose freely, without a story to justify it, is mind-blowingly liberating.

When we begin making choices in this way, we actually become better choice makers. Stripping away the justifications, we become more open to the pure impulses coming from a deeper place. And this is where the best choices are made.

PEACE IS FOUNDATIONAL

Peace is the foundation of happiness and a satisfying life. Without peace we are at the whim of our "monkey minds" and the endless clatter of the world around us. Finding a place of peace—of stillness and silence—within ourselves is job number one in life. All else flows from there.

When you read stories about people who are able to survive in horrific situations—warfare, concentration camps, survival challenges—with equanimity and grace, it is invariably because they were able to find a place of peace within themselves. On the other hand, we all know people whose lives are relatively comfortable but who live in a tortured or frantic state. They are at the whim of their noisy, busy minds.

If I had one piece of advice I could give to literally everyone, it would be this: every morning, when you wake up, get to a place of peace *before you do anything else*. Meditation, prayer, listening to calming music—there are many approaches you can use. But establish your inner peace *first*. *Then* read your emails, watch the news, get ready for work, etc. Try it. I guarantee life-changing results.

I have been doing yoga and meditation every day for the last thirty-five years. Every day—I'm not kidding. It is one of the foundational rituals of my life. It is like the air I breathe. I cannot start my day without this practice. I encourage you to find a practice that works for you … every day!

THE NEED FOR MENTORS AND MASTERS

Swami became a spiritual mentor for me in the years he was alive. But I have always had mentors. Mentors have served me remarkably well. A relationship with a person who has more experience and wisdom than you in a given area is invaluable. Mentorship lets you avoid countless mistakes and allows you to take the shortest path through challenges.

When I was starting out in business, I had Hillard Aronson. Such a gift.

When I was working around the est training, my mentors were the many talented trainers. Each one was exceptional, but Neal Mahoney (a.k.a. the Bear), in particular, trained me for two years in the trenches of Boston to be the leading training supervisor I would become.

For twenty-five years I have had Dan Sullivan as my entrepreneurial coach. Kim White has been my energy coach for the last five years. When people ask what an energy coach does, I respond simply,

"Kim eliminated all fear in my life, restored my spirit to God, and opened my ears to hear the angels when they are speaking to me." Any questions?

I've also had Peter Sias, of "Legacy" fame. Peter had worked for over ten years with Werner Erhard, the est trainers, and the est organization. He was the only person Werner allowed to use the "technology" and training of est. Marie introduced me to Peter four years ago, and I spent four full days, over a five-month period, working with Peter on something he called Legacy. The work asks the question, "What is the Legacy you want to *live in going forward*, not the one you want to leave behind?" Peter helped me discover my true ministry in life, which is "to ease people's pain and suffering about their money and guide them to live a life dedicated to their true passions." Peter's teaching stood on the shoulders of Werner, Hillard, Dan, and Kim and reset the sails of my life's journey.

In America we honor independence and the "self-made" person. We are suspicious of mentors and masters, as if having a mentor somehow makes us a "follower." This is especially true in the spiritual realm. The idea of following a master or guru is seen as brainwashing. As for me, I *relish* having a relationship with someone who is farther ahead on the path than I am. Whatever that path might be.

A great mentor/master doesn't try to create followers. They try to help you become your own master by building on the strengths you have inside. Everyone benefits, and we all fly higher.

EIGHT

YIELDING TO MY DREAMS

Mark Twain said the two greatest days in life are the day you are born and the day you find out why. It has taken me nearly sixty-five years to find that "why."

I started the book off with a very simple statement: "Do what you love, and the money will follow." (Remember that?) It sounds grand, doesn't it? It's what everyone wants. "So how do you actually make it happen, Charlie?" you may be asking. It's time to bring all the threads together.

I want to share with you how I finally came around to using *all* my gifts together in a way that I feel I am uniquely designed to do, among all eight billion souls currently roaming planet Earth. I want to also share how I came to find enduring peace in my life and a marriage that is everything my first marriage wasn't. The money part? That has always been relatively easy for me, thanks to the modeling I received early in life. But it is real and important nonetheless.

It all comes down to following my inner voice, rather than the patterns and prescriptions laid down by others. To paraphrase Robert Frost, each time two roads in the wood diverged, I took the one less traveled by—and that has made all the difference. And that is what I am urging you to do. Let me tell you how I've traveled these last few exciting miles.

FINAL MEETING WITH SWAMI

Swami gave me a tremendous gift. He brought peace into my life, against all odds. And so he became "my guy." I was all in with him. But I only saw him, physically, one additional time.

About a year after the first meeting, I got a call from Marie, asking me where I was. I told her I was in Texas, of all places—her home state.

"Well, I'm in California," she said. "In Joshua Tree. Swami's coming. And you need to be here."

Oy, here we go again. I told her I was leading a coaching workshop and that I had to get on a plane the next day.

Yeah, right. "You *need* to be here."

Sigh. I found a flight out of Texas to LA, and then a flight from LA to Palm Springs. My plane got in around twelve thirty or one in the morning. I rented a car and started driving up to Joshua Tree in the dark.

I was trying to get directions from Marie by phone, but there was no cell reception. So I got lost. I was on some remote desert road, going way below the speed limit. It was two in the morning, pitch dark, no lights, no signs. Suddenly, out of nowhere, blue police lights appeared in my rearview mirror. I pulled over, and an Asian American police officer, who had a touch of Swami in his eyes, approached my window.

He asked me if I was okay. I told him I was lost, and he gave me, essentially, a police escort all the way to Joshua Tree. Swami was watching out for me, even among all the devotees who had come to see him, and sent that particular officer to guide me.

When I pulled up at the venue, it looked like the Night of the Living Dead. A hundred people or more were wandering around the desert wrapped in blankets, holding prayer beads, at two in the morning. Marie came out to greet me at my car, and I asked her what was going on. She said, "Swami wants everyone to do their mantra for three hours before sleeping tonight."

I grinned at her through the window and said, in the voice of Swami, "Oh no, no mantra for me," wagging my finger at her.

I went to the check-in table, and the retreat people gave me the key to the room I would be sharing with another participant for the next three days. "Oh," they told me as I headed off to my room, "you need to do your mantra for three hours tonight."

I turned to her and said, "Oh no, no mantra for me."

I got to my room and met my roommate, a documentary filmmaker from London. He was sitting in his bed, doing his mantra. We chatted briefly and then he resumed his prayers. I climbed into bed and promptly said good night.

"What about your mantra?" he asked me.

"Oh no, no mantra for me."

The next morning I was up bright and early and well rested— unlike the mantra doers—and Marie and I were among the first to be allowed into the room where Swami was meeting with the retreat participants. This lack-of-mantra thing was working like a Disney World speed pass for me. I somehow jumped the line again. Swami spotted me and came over to greet me, and immediately we were laughing and telling jokes. Two bros.

MAYBE SOMETHING POSITIVE INSTEAD?

A seed was planted in me during that final weekend with Swami, which would later blossom into the project that has become my current life's work. During a session with Swami, I told him about a series of books I was planning to write, aimed at people going through divorces. The first book would be called *You Can Negotiate with Terrorists, but You Can't Negotiate with Your Soon-to-Be Ex-Wife.* The second book would be the same thing, only for women, and the third book would be lawyer horror stories from men *and* women.

Swami encouraged me not to write those books. "You might want to do something positive rather than negative," was how he succinctly put it.

Oh. He was right, of course. If I was going to pour my energy into a creative new project, it should be something that empowered the human spirit rather than fanned the flames of conflict. To use Swami's own words, "Our actions must leave a sweet fragrance."

I began to give serious thought to my mission in life. What was the true ministry I was born to carry forth? How could I leave a "sweet fragrance" in the world?

SWAMI DEPARTS

In 2012 Swami Kaleshwar left his body, as many advanced souls do. He was only in his forties, but he just lay down one day, and his consciousness departed for a higher plane.

All hell broke loose in his absence. His family members fought for control of his legacy and his "empire." Swami had a core group of disciples in the United States with whom the family went to war. But the problem was Swami himself had chosen his successor in the United States before he died—Monica Taylor, whom I mentioned in the last chapter and who is now a good friend of mine. Swami had also begun planning for the building of an ashram in the United States. On his last visit, he had toured various locations, looking for a place with the right kind of power and energy. He had finally found it on a mountaintop in Laytonville, California, way up in Mendocino County, surrounded by cannabis fields.

The work to build the ashram began after his death and continues today, in the location Swami chose. About fifteen devotees live full-time on the site in yurts. I have been heavily involved in the efforts. I bought the dump truck and steam shovel and other heavy equipment they're using. I'm funding the building of a shrine up there too. I never got a mantra, so I imagine a time in the future when hundreds of devotees will swarm the ashram every day. They'll all be dressed in saffron robes, and I'll be off to the side, the only guy in a business suit.

And Swami and I will be laughing. And I wouldn't have it any other way.

MY MINISTRY

One day I was visiting the ashram site and talking to Monica. We were sitting on the ground outside her yurt, talking about life, and suddenly things became crystal clear to me. I was sharing with her an idea I had to create a "one-man show." I wasn't yet clear on the details. I just knew I wanted to combine my twin talents as a financial advisor and as an entertainer.

She smiled her magical full-of-wisdom smile and said, "Charlie, I do believe we are in the same business."

"How so?" I asked.

"We are both in the business of easing people's pain and suffering in the world and guiding them to pursue their true passion and mission in life!"

Wow, I thought, *how true is that?* Peter Sias once asked me as I was going through Legacy, "Who would Charlie be if people weren't suffering?" (I actually have that question imprinted on a chair in my home office that I look at every day.) I said to Monica, "*My* ministry in life is to ease people's pain and suffering about their money, and *yours* is to ease their pain and suffering (period)."

Something clicked into place when I said that. And from that point on, my Yield of Dreams idea began to gather momentum, and I was on my way to finding out my "why."

YIELD OF DREAMS–IF YOU BUILD IT, THEY WILL COME...

After shutting down the 401(k) Coach business, I had taken a year or two to just meditate and enjoy life. I was still working in my financial business, but that was all. No theater, no bouncing around the country giving workshops. Slowly but surely, the "bug" started to bite again. I was ready to get back on the stage as a comic and an actor. And now I knew what my ministry was.

In January of 2019, I attended an event called the Abundance 360 Summit, run by a man named Peter Diamandis. It's a conference for leaders of highly successful companies that 360 people attend. The first thing I did was make a list of five people I wanted to connect with. Number one was a guy by the name of Mike Koenigs, a serial entrepreneur and a giant in the marketing industry.

The first event of day one was a networking session. I sat at an empty table, and as people started entering the room, a man came in and sat next to me. Who was it? Mike Koenigs, of course. Out of 360 people. I introduced myself and told him he was the guy I was hoping to meet. We became fast friends.

I told Mike I was considering getting back into performing and that I might even want to write a show. And so, over the next six months, we kicked ideas around. In June he reached out, telling me he had something he wanted to talk to me about.

"Charlie," he said, "all the great comics with TV shows, like Kimmel and O'Brien, hire comedy teams to help them write material. So here's the idea: I lock you in my condo in La Jolla, overlooking the Pacific ocean, with three comedians, me, and an amazing integrator named Marisa Brassfield [who had helped Peter Diamandis build Abundance 360]. And we'll see if we can create the show you want to create." In exchange for being producer of the show and receiving a six-figure check, Mike would find the comedians.

Now let's just pause for a moment as I ask you a very simple question.

How big a check would you write to a total stranger for the possibility of fulfilling a lifetime dream? Let's pause again and let that question sink in.

Hmm, I can see you are distracted by something and not fully taking in the gravity of the question.

So let me try it this way:

Imagine you were Dorothy in *The Wizard of Oz* meeting the wizard for the first time, or Luke Skywalker meeting Yoda, or Marty in *Back to the Future* meeting Christopher Lloyd's Dr. Emmett Brown and his time machine car. Is this starting to sink in? That's exactly who I was and who Mike Koenigs was (and is). He is the wizard, Yoda, and

Dr. Emmett Brown all rolled into one when it comes to amplifying someone's Unique Ability®!

THE LARGEST CHECK®

I had absolutely no evidence that Mike, let alone I, could make good on what he was proposing—that I would hole up in his Pacific Coast condo with three comedians who didn't know me from Adam, and at the end of the two days we would create something wondrous that would change my life and that of millions of others. Not a big ask, right?

But for me, a man who had been transformed by the best—my mentor Hillard, my transformer Werner Erhard, my entrepreneurial coach Dan Sullivan, my energy coach Kim White, my legacy leader Peter Sias, and my own guru Swami Kaleshar—yeah, I could suspend logic and go with the flow. Take a stand. Make a commitment. And pray, baby, pray.

In October of 2019, I boarded a plane from Bradley International to San Diego to begin what would become a three-year odyssey. A journey of wonderment, joy, laughter, play, and discovery for discovery's sake. I had no evidence that anything could happen, let alone magic. And yet in my heart of hearts—in my gut, in my spirit, in my soul—I just knew that this journey I was about to embark on was going to be eye-opening and successful beyond my wildest dreams. Look out, Alice, it was my turn down that rabbit hole.

Sitting in seat 2B next to me in first class for the first leg of my journey was a seventy-three-year-old guy. A guy I came to learn was astonishingly successful. He shared with me the many businesses he had built and sold and bought back and sold again for even more money. He shared photos of his mansion homes, his Ferrari, Lamborghinis, and vintage Bugatti race cars. Photos of him and his wife of fifty years traveling the world. The proud father and grandfather. This was Mr. Successful. Everything any entrepreneur would aspire to be.

Interesting, I thought to myself, as I made my way through the Atlanta airport to my connecting flight to San Diego, *that I would sit next to someone so incredibly successful.* "I wonder why?"

While boarding my flight to San Diego, I was on my headset negotiating a deal for a new car. As I was putting my bag in the overhead compartment, I glanced over to see who was sitting in 2C. It was a middle-aged man, dressed in a powder blue power suit, crisp white shirt, and shiny yellow tie. My new traveling companion, who must have overheard my phone conversation, looked up at me and said, "What kind of car are you buying?"

"Bentley," I responded as I slid in my seat. Nothing like a good ol' game of "power chess" to get things rolling.

Once in flight we began a five-and-a-half-hour conversation with almost no breaks. I learned that he was the CEO of a capital markets consulting firm. He was headed to San Diego to meet a major client for dinner, then fly back the next day to his home in Virginia, pick up his wife and daughter, and head to Genoa for two weeks of business and pleasure. This man was on the road almost every week of the year. He was no lightweight, business-wise.

When I told him about my financial background, he asked, "How do you get yield in this economic environment?" I shared a few financial strategies, but being the inquisitive coach, I sensed he was not happy with his work and his lot in life. And I told him so.

He responded, "I just turned fifty, and what I'd really like to do with my life is run a nonprofit and make an enormous impact in the world."

"Why not do it now?" I responded.

"Oh, no, no, no," he stammered. "I still need ten to twelve years to get the 'yield' on my portfolio in the right place and then … and then …" And he just looked out the window and let out a deep, long sigh. Here was this super successful man, still fairly young, exchanging his true passion in life for a job and paycheck that weren't taking him where his inner compass was directing him.

And what a contrast he was to my super successful companion on my first flight.

Why had God, Swami, and the angels put these two men next to me on those two flights as I made my way to meet my destiny in Mike's condo in La Jolla, California?

"Do what you love, and the money will follow," I thought as I lifted my luggage from the carousel and then waved down my Uber to head to Mike's. This odyssey was only nine hours old and was already getting interesting.

CREATING SOMETHING FROM NOTHING

That night I slept like a baby but woke up at five o'clock with my heart in my throat and pounding.

"I have nothing," a voice said in my head. "Nothing!"

It was true. I had paid Mike a king's ransom for the weekend. In less than four hours, I was going to meet my team of comedians and begin the process of figuring out what I truly wanted to create for my stage show. And I had … nothing.

Nothing written, no outline, no mission statement … zip.

What is a future king of the entertainment world to do?

Ask the universe! I crawled out of bed and went to the carpet in Mike's living room area to do what I have done every morning for the past thirty years—twenty minutes of yoga and fifteen minutes of meditation. This, I thought, would solve everything. Divine intervention would arrive on cue, and I would have one of those legendary bursts of inspiration to launch my journey.

The yoga was wonderful, the meditation peaceful, and the result … nothing.

Now what? It was six o'clock.

Well, how about a shower and shave? And a few extra prayers in the process.

Still nothing.

Finally, the solution came to me … coffee.

Yes, yes, I'll take a walk to the local Starbucks, get my favorite grande bone-dry coconut cappuccino, and the caffeine angels will arrive with the answers.

I began walking the short mile walk to Starbucks, singing with joy and laughter in my heart. The answers are at Starbucks, of course. Alas, there was no inspiration to be found in the coffee, but it still tasted amazing.

The answer must be in the ocean, then.

I made my way back from Starbucks and onto the beach across from Mike's condo.

There I set out to walk for thirty minutes and come face to face with divine inspiration.

And there is where I found … you guessed it, more nothing. Don't get me wrong—the sunrise, the crashing of the waves, and the surfers paddling out to meet their destiny were more than wonderful, but still …

No flash of light, no bolt of inspirational lightning.

I made my way back to Mike's condo to meet my comedians—and my fate—without a damn thing in hand, without so much as a seed of an idea for anyone to latch onto.

God help me, I thought, as the first knock hit the door, right at nine o'clock.

First, Marissa arrived, ever punctual. She was my "hope." I knew from my eight years of working with her at Abundance 360 that I would have one person in my corner, since she always laughed at my strange observational jokes. Then Mike arrived, the Man himself, with golden shining sneakers and that everything-is-going-to-work-out energy. (*What does he know? I'll show him.*) And then, one by one, my firing squad: my writing team of comedians. First, warm, silly-fun Jesse, then introspectively wise and amusing Ryan, and finally, via Zoom, the ever mystical and quirky Kyle.

My writing team was complete. Now what?

After some brief introductions and a process Dan Sullivan calls the positive focus, where everyone shares something positive that recently happened in their personal or work life.

I looked at "the boys" and said, "So let me ask you a question. What were you each thinking when Mike said, 'Hey how would you like to spend two days holed up in my condo with some old white Jewish financial advisor and try to make money funny?'"

Well, that got things going. Sideways, at first.

"The boys" spent the next two hours asking me what I wanted to accomplish.

"Do you want to do a financial seminar?"

"No," I said.

"Do you want to do money webinars?"

"No."

"Videos on financial topics?"

"No." I paused. "Boys, I want to go back and do stand-up, but on money topics that will change the way people view money."

I shared everything I had done and created as a financial advisor, a stand-up comedian, and an actor/entertainer. I shared my book *Paychecks for Life*, my Desirement playing cards, the fifteen money myths I have identified that hold people back from pursuing their true passions ...

And then ...

I started to tell stories.

I shared with them how I had met Mr. Successful-and-Fulfilled on my flight from Bradley to Atlanta and Mr. Successful-but-Unfulfilled on my flight from Atlanta to San Diego.

I shared about my favorite movie, *Field of Dreams*, and how I had seen it a hundred times and still cried in all the same places. How that movie was filled with characters longing for something they really wanted in life. How each one of them, from Shoeless Joe to Doc to Ray Kinsella, had to give up something big in their lives for their real dreams to come true.

And then the bolt of lightning hit, and what a bolt it was.

At 11:13 a.m. the introspective, wise, and amusing Ryan said, "I have the title of your show: *Yield of Dreams!*"

And we were off to the races.

I started to act out all the stories of my life and the observations I had made in my financial business over the past forty years. My acting and storytelling capabilities were energized by the comedians and the collaborative relationship we quickly created. A key success ingredient was that everyone left their egos at the door. By the end of the two days, the walls of Mike's condo were covered with huge sticky-note papers filled with the many stories of my life, organized into a full-length one-man show.

We went from N-O-T-H-I-N-G to "Oh my God, I think we have something here, boys!"

I flew home from La Jolla with my suitcase stuffed with those sticky notes and the beginning of a script Marissa Brassfield had cobbled together as the comedians, Mike, and I spitballed ideas for those forty-eight hours.

As part of Mike's genius, he used a tool called Otter to capture both the text and the audio of every conversation we had those two days. So nothing was missed—the good, the bad, or the ugly. It's all fodder for potential creativity, as people in show biz know.

I then spent the next eight weeks writing the bulk of the show—116 pages just poured out of me. Every story, every crazy idea, every riff of my life came out like a flood.

I then handed that torrent of free-flowing ideas back to the team. Kyle, Ryan, and Jesse worked till December to organize it into a script we could begin editing.

I flew back to San Diego in January of 2020 to hole up for two more days with the team and rework our rough script into a tighter and more credible show.

And then … COVID-19.

THE UNKNOWN–DOUBTING YOUR DOUBTS!

None of us had any clue what we were in for—and by "none of us," I mean the entire world! And when faced with the unknown, most people give in. They simply stop reaching for their big dreams and begin to catalog all the reasons they cannot succeed …

"I'm not good enough," "I don't have enough talent, time, money," "When I was three, my parents divorced" … Fill in the blank. The voice of doubt takes over, barking and nipping at us, reminding us why we can't succeed at whatever we're passionate about.

My advice is if you want to doubt something, why not doubt your doubts? You made them up. They're not real. If you empower your doubts by believing them, you will find evidence in the world that they are real.

On the other hand, if you question your doubts, you will find evidence in the world that they are *not* real. This is your true "superpower" power as a human being—the power to choose against your doubts and then find support in the world for creating your purpose and passion, from absolutely *nothing*!

Instead of indulging the monkey mind, simply say every day, "Mind, thank you for sharing all the reasons you doubt my ability to achieve what I want most in life. Now, I will proceed to do what I need to do to accomplish my dreams."

COVID was my greatest test. The world came to a screeching halt. No one knew what was happening or whether we would all survive this threat to mankind. Half the world rolled up into a ball, hunkered down, and stopped living their lives. The other half, the entrepreneurial half, said, "Wow, what an incredible opportunity this is. How can I take advantage of it?"

GO THE DISTANCE

In *Field of Dreams*, Kevin Costner's character, Ray Kinsella, is tested. He is a man in pain, longing for redemption from his father, longing to tell him one more time that he loves him.

One day a voice in his cornfield whispers, "Ease his pain … Go the distance." Ray is instructed to mow down his cornfields—his only source of income—to build his "field of dreams."

At first Ray is confused, but he follows the voice and takes up the seemingly insane challenge. The townspeople think Ray has lost it. There is absolutely no evidence to suggest that he will succeed in his quest. He goes on a "hero's journey," just like Dorothy, Luke Skywalker, and Marty McFly.

And he is rewarded beyond his wildest dreams.

During COVID I decided to "go the distance." I built my own video studio in my office building, with a green screen, two cameras, two video screens, and lighting, to help me work on the show. Spent $50,000, with absolutely no assurance I would succeed. I was not going to let a little thing like COVID stop me.

And COVID tried. I've had it twice. The first time was in April of 2020 before the medical community really knew what it was. And it got me good—fever of 103 for ten days. Every day it felt like a different mob, armed with baseball bats, had come to attack a different part of my body. Meat sweats for eight days. And then the fatigue for three weeks.

I got it again in January of 2021.

Undaunted, I continued my quest to stage my show. The comedians and I worked by Zoom from February to July of 2020, fine-tuning the script. Then I decided it was time to start rehearsing the show, preparing for the day the world would reopen and I could find a live venue in which to perform.

I reached out to a very dear and old friend of mine, the talented actress and director Susan Daniels. Susan had directed me in *Crossing Delancey* and *Lost in Yonkers* at Mount Holyoke Summer Theater in the early '90s. When I first shared with her the idea of the show, she was hesitant to get involved. So I sent her the script, and once she read it, she was inspired and came on board as my director. She then recommended a stage manager, Carly Della Penna, who quickly learned how to operate the studio cameras and sound. Via Zoom, Susan and

I met for the next eight months, twice a week, to refine the show and get it on its feet, as we all waited for the world to reopen its doors.

THE 4 C'S FORMULA®–COMMITMENT, COURAGE, CONFIDENCE, AND CAPABILITY

My entrepreneurial coach Dan Sullivan has a wonderful tool he calls The 4 C's Formula®. It is a way to focus your mind on succeeding at any project you are working on.

Step one: commitment. When you truly commit 100 percent of your mind, body, and spirit to something you are passionate about, "Providence and the heavens move in alignment."

The famous poem "On Commitment" (attributed to Goethe) says it best:

Until one is committed, there is hesitancy,

the chance to draw back,

always ineffectiveness.

Concerning all acts of initiative and creation,

there is one elementary truth,

the ignorance of which kills

countless ideas and splendid plans:

that the moment one definitely commits oneself,

then providence moves too.

All sorts of things occur to help one

that would never otherwise have occurred.

A whole stream of events issues from the decision,

raising to one's favor all manner of unforeseen incidents

and meetings and material assistance

which no man could have dreamed

would come his way.

Whatever you can do or dream you can,

begin it.

Boldness has genius, power and magic in it.

What started to happen to me once I committed to staging my one-man show—in the face of COVID and the many doubters in my life—was that providence began to move in my favor.

Step two: courage. Most people don't have the courage of their convictions and the "grit" to stand in the face of the naysayers. But when you are looking into the void, courage is an essential trait. Courage will overcome all obstacles. Courage will carry you through the darkness and out into the light. During COVID I used courage to stay on the right path, even though I had no evidence to support me.

Step three: confidence. With commitment and courage, your confidence goes through the roof. It begins to accelerate and becomes an elixir for everyone you come in contact with. Strangers with talent beyond yours start to show up at your doorstep, wanting to support your passion and purpose.

Step four: capabilities. The biggest lesson I've learned as both an entrepreneur and actor is that you can't do it alone. If you want to grow, if you want to achieve great things in your life, you must surround yourself with people who are more gifted and talented than you are in all the areas you suck at. Dan Sullivan calls this Unique Ability® Teamwork, and I have subscribed to it for twenty-five years. I've built and successfully sold two companies for seven and eight figures. I've built and successfully sold a community bank. And I've successfully created my own one-man show. None of these things could I have done without the unique talents and abilities of the individuals I have surrounded myself with.

Dan is fond of saying that as a business leader you are either "in charge" or "in control." You can only be one. Most people in business want to be "in control," which leads to micromanaging everyone, for fear someone will screw up. Or worse, you adopt the belief that no one can do anything better than you or that it's easier to just do it yourself.

To be super successful and create success and growth for others, you need to be "in charge."

I like to say, in both my financial business and my performance work, I am in control of nothing and in charge of everything. I'm like Teddy Roosevelt riding up San Juan Hill with the Spaniards shooting down at me. I'm leading the charge, and my "capability team" of employees and collaborators are all inspired to charge up the hill with me, in spite of the extreme circumstances. But they all know more than I do in their unique ways.

Once you have made the commitment and found the courage of your convictions, your confidence will expand, and the angels will bring the capabilities (your Unique Ability team) to your doorstep.

Here are just a few examples of the "unforeseen incidents, meetings, and material assistance" that I could never have dreamed would come my way but that have made all the difference in my success.

THE MAGIC OF PROVIDENCE

In December of 2019, before COVID struck, my son Noah and I were in Park City, Utah, for his winter break, skiing. We were visiting a dear friend of mine, Kenny Bretschneider. Kenny is the twenty-first-century version of Walt Disney. He created Evermore Park in Pleasantville, Utah, an amazing immersive experience (in which my wife Lorie and I are investors). He made his fortune creating and selling something known as the VOID 4D experience.

Across the street from Evermore, Kenny has a three-level Formula One racetrack. Noah and I enjoyed a few spins around the track, and while we were there, Kenny introduced us to Sean D. Reyes, the attorney general of Utah. When I introduced myself, Sean whimsically said, "Any relations?" I responded with a smile, "You're only the fiftieth person to ask me that question today." He was referring to Jeffrey Epstein, the infamous sexual predator who was prominently featured in the news at that time. Sean's response was not what I expected. He said, "You know, *we* caught him!" Turns out, Epstein was running an underground network of underage women through Utah to Florida. Along with the now famous FBI agent, Tim Ballard, Reyes helped apprehend Epstein. Okay, interesting enough story. But nothing to do with me, right?

Well, in January of 2022, Dan Sullivan said to me, "Charlie, you should make a documentary of the making of *Yield of Dreams.*" (*What a great idea*, I thought.) "And I've got the guy who can do it for you: Nick Nanton, an Emmy Award–winning documentary filmmaker." Within two weeks I was on a Zoom call with Dan as he introduced Nick and me to each other.

As Nick and I were waiting for Dan to join the call, I saw above Nick, on his shelf, a set of sixteen—count 'em—gold Emmy statues. I asked Nick, "Where are you located?" He told me he was in his office outside of Orlando. I said, "That's interesting. My son Noah goes to Full Sail University in Winter Park, Florida, and I'm heading down this weekend to see him …"

Nick's response was another one of Goethe's unforeseen incidents. He said, "My office is on the *campus* of Full Sail, and the founders are good friends of mine. Why don't you and Noah come over Saturday night, and we can hang out and get to know each other?"

That weekend Noah and I paid a visit to Nick and his family. Nick has an amazing home on a lake outside Winter Park. The back of the house has a pool, jacuzzi, basketball court, batting dock, and lounge area, complete with multiple TVs, a huge bar, and a grill. Pure fun and entertainment. Noah immediately gravitated to Nick's kids, and Nick and I sat down to a great bottle of wine and cigars.

The stage was set for something magical. As we were chatting, telling stories, and getting to know each other, for some reason I felt compelled to tell Nick the story of meeting Sean Reyes. Nick surprised me by saying, "Oh, I know Sean."

"You know Sean Reyes, the attorney general of the state of Utah?"

"Yeah," Nick went on, "Sean called me last year and said, 'How would you like to film a raid in Haiti as we try to capture some bad guys doing bad things with underage girls?'"

What? my mind shouted in disbelief. What were the chances of this connection? I looked at Nick and simply said, "I don't know who you are ... but you're making my documentary film!" And we were off to the races.

Over the course of the next nine months, as COVID continued, Nick, his film crew, and I shot at locations all over the country, from the *Field of Dreams* field in Dyersville, Iowa, to Swami's ashram on the mountaintop in Laytonville, California, to my homes in Massachusetts and Connecticut to a dinner where all my oldest and dearest friends and classmates roasted me. (You can watch the documentary of the making of *Yield of Dreams* on my website, www.yieldofdreams.live. We were fortunate enough to win a Silver Telly Award for marketing of the show.)

But wait, there's more.

As I was rehearsing the show in my studio, I realized we needed graphics to augment my stories. I reached out to Nick, who suggested I contact JL Briggs down in Florida. JL and I jumped on a Zoom call in February of 2021. I asked about his background, and what he told me knocked me off my chair—literally.

JL said, "Charlie, I grew up and went to school in your area. I graduated from college in 1983 and went to work as an agent selling life insurance for the MassMutual agency in New Hampshire."

"What?" I blurted out. "Ed Mullen's agency?"

"Yep."

My God, this was my twin brother from another mother. His career path was a duplicate of mine back in 1979.

I said, "JL, I don't know who you are, but I don't need to teach you anything about the financial side of my business. You're my graphic designer!"

There are a half dozen more of these Goethe-esque "streams of events" that issued from my commitment to make *Yield of Dreams* happen, "raising to my favor all manner of unforeseen incidents and meetings and material assistance which I could never have dreamed."

The last one I'll mention here is how I met Tony Castrigno and Mark Rubinsky, the executive producers of *Yield of Dreams.*

As I was rehearsing in my studio and traveling with Nick's crew filming the documentary, I started to ponder the question, "How the f**k am I going to *stage* this show once the world opens up?"

I'm a big believer in putting your ideas out into the world, so the world has a chance to tell you if you're on the right track or not. So I started sharing what I was up to with everyone I knew. Most people do the opposite. They keep their best ideas to themselves for fear someone will steal them or, worse, tell them their ideas are bad. Not I.

In November of 2020, when the world was just starting to open up again, I was in Dallas, Texas, having dinner with dear clients of mine, Larry Leon and Lori Darley. Larry asked what I was up to, and I immediately started talking about the show. I said, "I'm getting to the point where I have to figure out how to get this thing on its feet, which takes an entire production crew—lighting designers, sound people, tech crews ... an army!"

Larry smiled and said, "Why don't I introduce you to my friend Tony Castrigno and his partner Mark Rubinsky? They're producers out of New York City." Ask, and ye shall receive. A month later I was on a Zoom call with Mark and Tony, and they became my executive producers in March 2021. Without these two gentlemen, *Yield of Dreams* would never have seen the light of day. During the next six months, they worked to bring together the army of extremely talented individuals who would become my production crew. (I've listed these amazing unique ability team members that made *Yield of Dreams* a success, in the appendix of this book.)

THE SHOW OPENS

On August 27 and 28, I walked onto the stage we created at the Northampton Arts Center to deliver my first stage performance in nineteen years. Over two hundred friends, clients, and strangers sat through the first iteration of *Yield of Dreams*, a one-hour-and-forty-minute hodgepodge of storytelling, stand-up, and financial education. Yes, I received a standing ovation both nights and some amazing feedback.

Most special was the fact that my ninety-three-year-old mother, Margaret Cecile Epstein, was there in the front row with my nephew, Michael Epstein, to witness the birth of my return to live theater. And for that I will forever thank the angels.

With 135 feedback surveys in hand, Tony, Mark, and I then set out to rewrite the show. Once again Tony and Mark came through by delivering to my doorstep one of the most amazing playwrights working today. It has been my pleasure to know and work with Jenny Lynn Bader, an actress herself. From December of 2021 right up through the opening of the revised version of *Yield of Dreams* on June 24, 25, and 26, 2022, at the Leslie Phillips Theater on the campus of Holyoke Community College (where I am a trustee), Jenny worked tirelessly to recraft the show into a journey of how I have been able to bring my two personas, Charlie Epstein, the financial advisor, and Charles Burtaine, the actor and performer, together into one cohesive person. Jenny has taught me so much about the art of acting and performing what is on the page.

Tony and Mark also reconfigured the entire production team. I loved working with Susan Daniels, my first director, but as a lifelong learner, I wanted to work with a new director to challenge me as an actor. Tony and Mark introduced me to David Ruttura, who did just that for me. Our production crew even consisted of a Tony Award–winning lighting designer. (I've listed everyone involved in the revised production in the appendix.)

BROADWAY BECKONS

After the June performances (which, as of this writing, were only a month ago), people asked me what the most satisfying aspects were of performing the show.

First, there was/is the pure challenge of it all. I have never in my life been so frightened of doing anything as I was of performing this last version of the show. To you, my dear reader, I say emphatically, if you are not doing something that scares the shit out of you, you are not living your life to its fullest!

Second has been the audience's feedback, which has been over-whelmingly positive.

After Friday night's performance, my director David's fiancée Katie said, "I didn't know what to expect. The show touched me on all three levels—spiritually, emotionally, and financially—and I have never had that experience from live theater in my life."

For Saturday evening's performance, all my first cousins, along with my sister, her husband, and my son Noah were in attendance. My mother, in Swami fashion, had chosen to leave her body three months earlier, and the family was in town that weekend for her memorial service the following morning. The afternoon before the show, I realized that in my entire sixty-four years, not one of my cousins, nor my sister, nor my son, for that matter, had ever seen me perform. Well, if I wasn't scared enough, that just added fuel to the fire.

At the end of Saturday's performance, my oldest cousin, Dr. Jeff Burtaine, whom I adore but who can be a bit, um, "prickly," put his arm around my shoulder, looked me in the eyes, and said, "I don't know what it takes to do what you just did, other than thousands and thousands of hours of practice. I had no idea what an amazing performer my baby cousin was. Here's what I compare it to: imagine you've been hanging out with a guy for forty years, and one day you ask him, 'Oh, by the way, what's your name?' and he says, 'Lebron James!'" Wow.

ONE LAST *WOW* MOMENT

In the audience Saturday night was a Broadway producer and friend of mine, Alan Shorr. No lightweight, Alan had just won his first Tony Award for producing *The Lehman Trilogy* on Broadway. After the show Alan came up to me and said, "Charlie, I had no idea what an amazing actor and performer you are. It just so happens I'm producing *42nd Street* at the Goodspeed Opera House (in Connecticut) this fall. We're planning to take the show to Broadway in 2023. There's an actor we've been trying to get for a role that you would be perfect for. I just called my partner Richard and told him if the actor doesn't sign by tomorrow, I just found the actor to do the role!"

Slam-drop my microphone!

I just love Goethe.

NEXT STOP: NATIONAL TOUR, NETFLIX SPECIAL, AND A REALITY TV SHOW

And now the question beckons: Where to go from here?

What about you? What are your grand plans for your life and a bigger future?

I, for one, have grand plans for *Yield of Dreams*.

First, a thirty-city national tour. I want to get my message out to millions to pursue their passion and find their purpose in life. Too many people are working in a job they hate for a paycheck they hope will one day give them enough security to retire and do what they want, at least till the angels show up, saying, "Time's up—we're coming for you!"

That's what I call dying, not living.

As I say in my show, the biggest myth we human beings have about money is "it will make you happy and solve all your problems." That is a false belief. Don't get me wrong—it's great to have money. But only as a utility to support your purpose and passion. *Now.*

Remember Mark Twain's statement, "The two greatest moments in your life are the day you're born and the day you find out why."

At the end of my show, I look out at the audience and say, "I finally figured out why I'm here on this stage in front of all of you: to ease your pain and suffering about your money. That's my passion and my purpose."

I'm still tweaking and iterating the show and, for that matter, my life.

ONWARD AND UPWARD

Nick Nanton's crew filmed the first two nights, and I'm planning to livestream the show beginning in the fall of 2022.

I'm creating a metaverse version, where people can put on their Oculus goggles and experience the show in an immersive way.

The goal is to get a million followers and then knock on the door of Netflix, Amazon, Hulu, and the other big TV-streaming services with a series pitch. We also plan to use the show to generate clients for the financial planning business at a whole new level.

In short, the sky's the limit.

I couldn't be more excited. And I couldn't be more *satisfied*, knowing this show's blend of humor, storytelling, audiovisual stimulation, financial/life advice, and sheer audacity is something no one else on the planet could do but me. I gave oxygen to my dreams, and now my show will be giving oxygen to other people's dreams.

Yippee. Om. And let's roll.

ON THE HOME FRONT–PERSONAL SATISFACTION TRUMPS EVERYTHING

I don't want to end this book without also sharing the incredible transformation that has taken place in my personal life and relationships. I am now in a joyous marriage with my lifelong partner, Lorie. Our relationship is off-the-charts honest, open, respectful, loving, and empowering. We work together, laugh together, and cry together. And for two people who are complete opposites, we enjoy doing endless things together.

Lorie likes to say her first marriage of twenty-five years was extreme market research. And I like to say my marriage of twenty-five years was *severe* market research. The "research" paid off for both of us.

Lorie and I first met in a way that is straight out of a Hollywood rom-com. The universe literally hurled us at each other. I was in a parking lot, walking away from my car, and Lorie was backing up in her Jeep. She rammed into me, knocking me to the ground.

The line she said next was right out of a Hollywood movie too. She rolled her window down, looked back at me, and said, "You're not a lawyer, are you?"

I am fond of saying, "God put a slow hit on me that day … it just took several years for it to materialize!"

As I was picking myself up off the ground, I informed her I was not a lawyer but rather in the financial services business.

She said, "Oh, I'm in between jobs and I need to roll my 401(k) over."

"They call me the 401(k) Coach."

Never one to miss a sale, I hobbled over to my car and grabbed a promotional cassette with my picture on it—my "audio business card." I gave it to her and said, "Here, crazy lady. Listen to this and then call my office," and limped off to the appointment I was now late for.

About a month later, I was standing in the lobby—we both worked in the same building—and I saw her coming toward the elevator.

"You're not going to run me over again, are you?"

She apologized profusely again and told me she hadn't called me back because she didn't think she qualified as a client. I told her we would take care of her anyway, and that was how we met. At the time, though, she was still married, and so was I, so nothing developed. But a couple of years later, she called my office. She was getting divorced and needed to buy some life insurance to cover her son, who was twelve.

I was at the end of my marriage too. And the rest is beautiful history.

I love our relationship. We look at the world completely differently, but what I've now learned is not to try to change other people. I accept Lorie completely as she is. And in doing so, I find I love everything about her, *especially* the things that drive me crazy. Have you ever heard the Luke Combs song, "Beautiful Crazy"? That captures my feelings perfectly, in particular the line, "Her crazy's beautiful to me." Every day gives me something new to appreciate.

· · ·

I am blessed indeed in my life. I have a beautiful marriage and beautiful homes. I have children and stepchildren and grandchildren I love and admire. I have a treasure chest of great personal friendships with people I have known since I was five years old—what a gift. I have financial security and plenty of money. I have a thriving business and some great commercial property ventures. I'm having a blast with my one-man show and my other creative projects—such as this book! I don't take credit for the blessings life has given me. But I do take credit for one thing: for opening the door to let those blessings in. And the way I have done that is by doing what I love. Not by playing it safe or following someone else's script.

Open *your* door. Do it now, not later. Find your passion and your purpose. Surround yourself with people more talented than you, and inspire and challenge them to grow and take risks.

Fail fast, fail forward, and fail often.

We all have a quiet, insistent voice inside us, urging us in the direction of our dreams. This is the same voice that guides the monarch butterflies on their migratory journey and tells the improv musician which chord to play next. It is the voice Ray Kinsella heard in *Field of Dreams*, telling him, "If you build it, they will come." This voice flows from the part of us that is connected to the heart of reality—to God—and it urges us to play the unique role we alone were designed to play. When we do that, we not only find joy and satisfaction for ourselves; we give our gifts fully to the world. And the world is better for it. This I know in every fiber of my being.

WHAT I LEARNED ALONG THE WAY

Some final thoughts from this present chapter of my life …

LIFE IS WONDERMENT, JOY, LAUGHTER, PLAY, AND DISCOVERY FOR DISCOVERY'S SAKE

No need to explain further. Every day this is what I remind myself to live for: wonderment, joy, laughter, play, and discovery for discovery's sake. Anything less, why bother? Anything *else*, why bother?

LIFE IS "BEAUTIFUL CRAZY"; TREAT IT THAT WAY

Something my present marriage has taught me is that two people can celebrate one another in all their flaws and differences without trying to change each other. This principle, I've come to realize, applies virtually everywhere else in life too.

A garden is made up of many different kinds of plants and flowers. It's not all marigolds or all geraniums. So too with the "garden of humanity." We are better off, individually and collectively, when we all live our uniqueness and let others do the same.

These days people around the world have become obsessed with making themselves right and other people wrong. A new tribalism is sweeping the globe, a driving desire to turn "the others" into bad guys and glorify our own point of view.

Stay away from that, I say. Give up the idea of changing the minds and behaviors of people around you. Focus all your energy on being the truest version of *you* that you can be. Nothing else is required of you. Period.

By doing so you will attract other like-minded individuals who crave what you crave and desire what you desire—to keep growing and learning and discovering for discovery's sake.

Just by being yourself and appreciating others for who they are, you will do more to lower the temperature in today's world than by any efforts to promote whatever point of view you think is "right." I'm not saying you should stop expressing your beliefs and convictions. Of course not. I'm just saying give up the idea that it's your job to change others. It isn't.

When you learn to appreciate the "beautiful crazy" in others, you learn to appreciate it in yourself. And in doing so, you give yourself permission to be the fullest version of who you are.

And I, for one, can't wait to see that.

CONTINUE THE JOURNEY WITH CHARLIE

Scan the QR code below
to stream the *Yield of Dreams* live show!

Scan the QR code below
to pick up a deck of *Desirement Cards*!

Scan the QR code below
for the *Myths of Money* workbook!

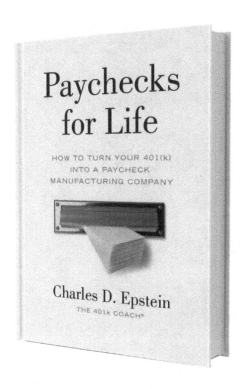

Scan the QR code below
for the *Paychecks for Life* audiobook.